What this Book is all about

This book is written for one purpose only:

To give you the **skills** and knowledge to administrate your firewall in the **fastest way** with a solid theoretical foundation

It does not cover every topic, only those that are needed for you to get around quickly and administrate your firewall in different topologies and use cases

Every chapter includes hands-on practices

It is written for **beginners and intermediate users**

The following book will help you to get around and feel cosy with your FortiGate firewall for most everyday tasks:

Configuring Interfaces, firewall address objects, static routes, policies, understand the different sessions that are created and terminated, and the Logs that will help you to understand your network behaviour

Table Of Contents

Basic Setup

Welcome to "Fortigate Admin Crash Course

Everything in this book is done on a virtual machine, which you can download at https://support.fortinet.com/

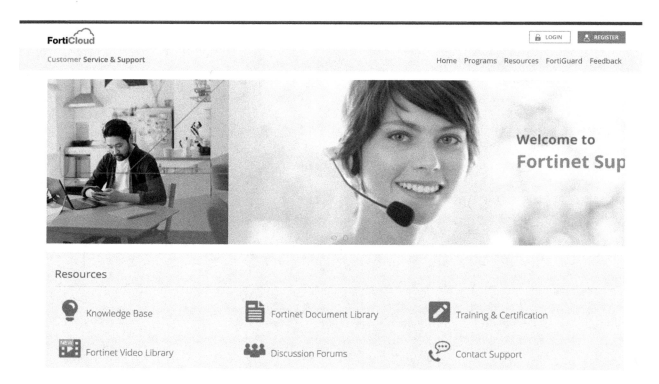

Here you will create a free account, once you set up your account, navigate to the **Download** section at the top bar and click on **VM Images**

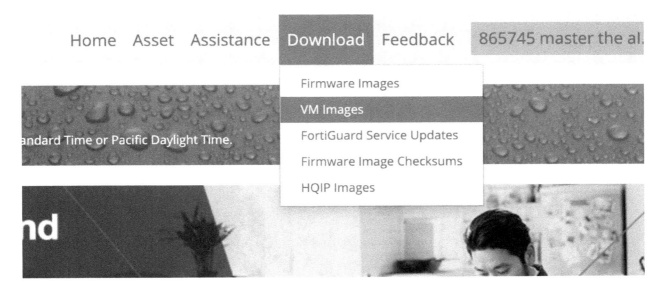

You will find different virtual machines images, choose your VM platform, I use the **VMware ESXi** with my VMware fusion for Mac

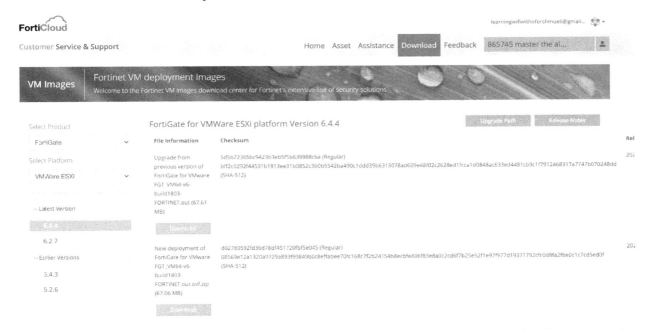

Make sure that you download the correct image (new deployment) . the current version, at the time this book was written, is **6.4.4**

The free version that you will download has some limitations, but it will do for most of our practices

Importing your **VM**

Importing the image to your VM platform and configuring your FortiGate depends on your OS of choice, we will do it using My Macbook, but the flow is very similar in windows

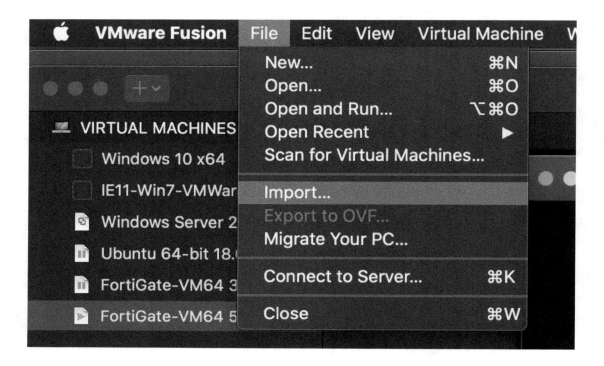

Go to **File --- Import** and choose your Fortigate VM that you have just downloaded. The download is usually in ZIP, so you will have to extract it

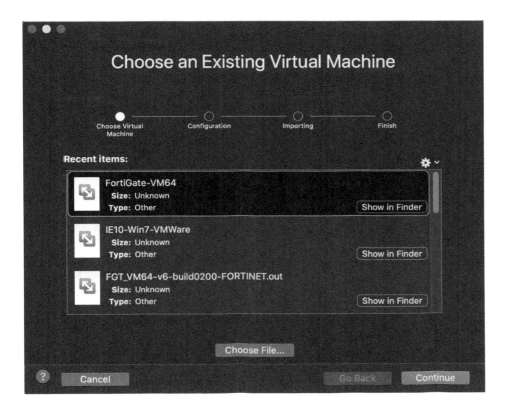

The setup should take a few minutes

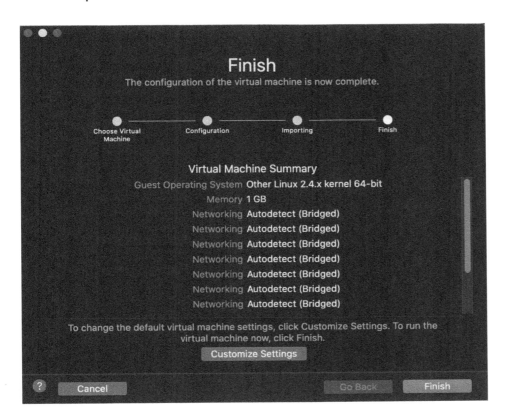

Once you finish the setup, you will see your VM summary. Press the Finish button, and your VM will start to load and Booting the Kernel

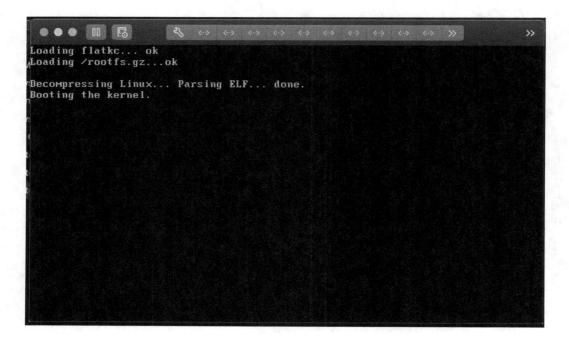

When that finishes, you will be prompt to enter your credentials

Enter **"admin"** (lower case) for the user name

And enter a password, you will be asked to re-enter it

```
● ● ●  ⏸  🖳       🔧  ⟨·⟩ ⟨·⟩ ⟨·⟩ ⟨·⟩ ⟨·⟩  »          📷 FortiGate-VM64 6    ⬜

Loading flatkc... ok
Loading /rootfs.gz...ok

Decompressing Linux... Parsing ELF... done.
Booting the kernel.

System is starting...
Interface mapping (E1000)
Serial number is FGVMEVHE5Z9B9L13

FortiGate-VM64 login: admin_
```

The following are Command-line commands, that you don't need to understand,
for now, we will set up the interface that will connect us to the Management page
through the browser

```
FortiGate-VM64 # config system interface

FortiGate-VM64 (interface) # edit port1

FortiGate-VM64 (port1) # set mode static

FortiGate-VM64 (port1) # set ip 10.0.3.78/24

FortiGate-VM64 (port1) # set allowaccess http https

FortiGate-VM64 (port1) # end

FortiGate-VM64 #
```

The IP address that you have just configured is a static one, make sure that it is
in your home/office subnet , the one that you are connected to

The **"set allowaccess"** actually defines the protocols that you are allowed to
connect through as an admin

Now open up your browser, using the address you have configured, and enter the credentials you have set up at the beginning (**admin, password**)

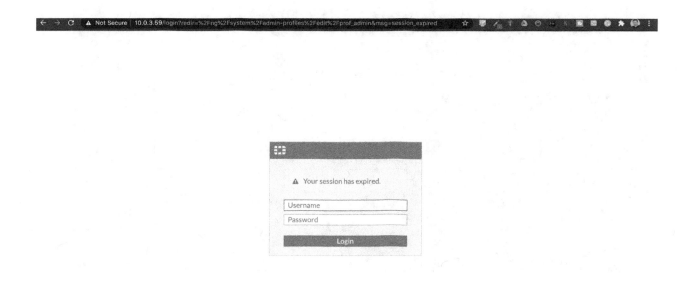

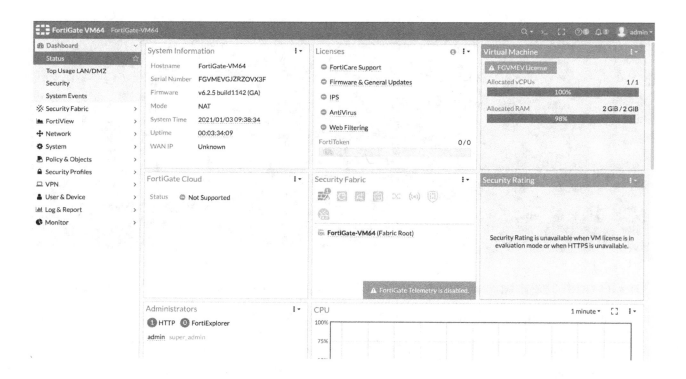

Physical **appliance**

On a physical device, the port1 interface is usually configured with a DHCP server (more on the different services later on) and an IP address of 192.168.1.99.

You will need to connect your computer to that port. you can also configure your computer in the 192.168.1.0 subnet range (configure it with a static IP address in that range if it doesn't get for some reason an IP address from port1 interface) **All of the things that you will learn in this book applies to both Virtual and physical devices**

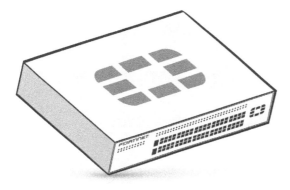

Let's Start

You can do a lot with your NGFW firewall, from Simple Rules, Web filtering, Deep SSL inspection of the traffic, IPsec tunnels, custom IPS signatures, even using it as a web application firewall. This book will focus on most used administration topics, as well as firewall rules, routing and analyzing sessions

We will look at the different capabilities, using screenshots from my home FortiGate but let's start with the basic things you do when you connect through the administrative interface and that is:

- Set admin profile
- Set up new interfaces for your LAN
- Config firewall address objects, for users, machines, anything in your LAN, that you may need to address
- Configure a default static route that will allow anyone to get out to the internet through your WAN port
- Configure your first policy

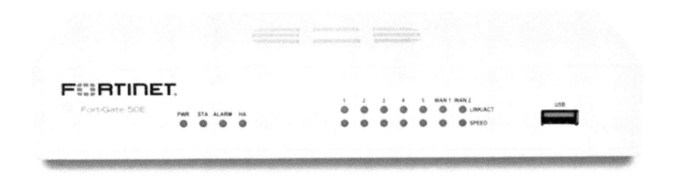

We will configure the above using the Graphical user interface, but we will focus on the **Command Line**, which is the best way to get into the advanced stuff.

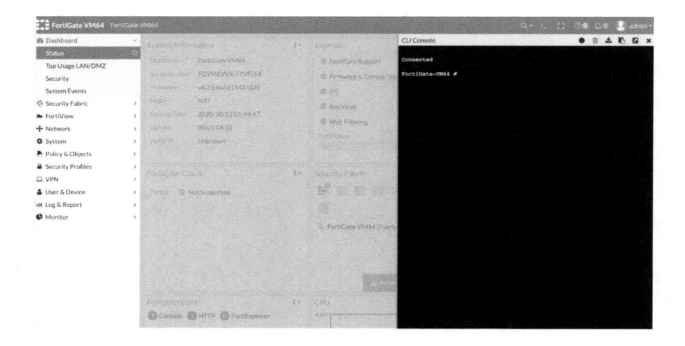

Once you are connected to your FortiGate for the first time (On one of the available ports), you are actually the Administrator of the machine. you have all the ROOT privileges and you can do just about anything from assigning new administrators or configuring your FortiGate firewall without any limitations

On your Left menu pane click **system--- administrators**, choose **admin and edit** you can configure your admin profile (password and name), 2-factor authentication, trusted hosts (IP addresses) that you can connect from, and more

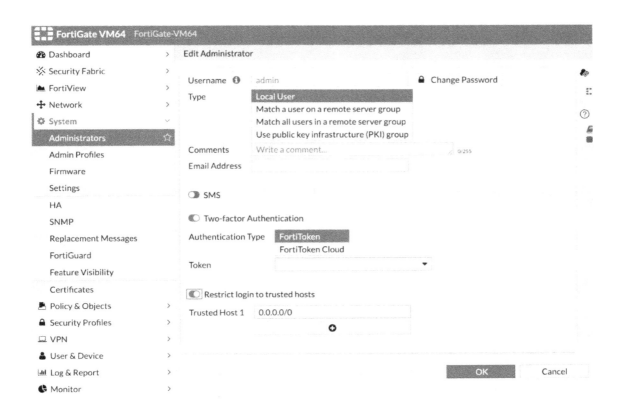

FortiGate VM64 FortiGate-VM64

- 🌐 Dashboard   ›
- ⚙ Security Fabric   ›
- 📊 FortiView   ›
- ✛ Network   ›
- ⚙ System   ⌄
  - **Administrators**   ☆
  - Admin Profiles
  - Firmware
  - Settings
  - HA
  - SNMP
  - Replacement Messages
  - FortiGuard
  - Feature Visibility
  - Certificates
- 🛡 Policy & Objects   ›
- 🔒 Security Profiles   ›
- 🖥 VPN   ›
- 👤 User & Device   ›
- 📊 Log & Report   ›
- 🌐 Monitor   ›

Edit Administrator

Username ❶	admin
Type	**Local User**
	Match a user on a remote server group
	Match all users in a remote server group
	Use public key infrastructure (PKI) group
Comments	Write a comment... 0/255
Email Address	

🔒 Change Password

◯ SMS

◉ Two-factor Authentication

Authentication Type   **FortiToken**
           FortiToken Cloud

Token   ▼

◉ Restrict login to trusted hosts

Trusted Host 1   0.0.0.0/0

➕

[OK]   [Cancel]

Configuring an Admin Account

You are the Admin of your Firewall, similar to ROOT in a Linux Machine

Configuring an admin profile is probably one of the first things that you will do with your FortiGate.

You can set up your admin profile using the graphical user interface, and you will probably do so once you get into your FortiGate. But this time, we'll do it using the command line.

Looking at the different admin profiles, we can see that there are two main profiles.

Super and **Professional**

The first profile is the **super admin**, which actually has permissions to just about anything, it has the **Read/Write** permissions to any place in the FortiGate interface. The second profile is the **professional admin**. which is usually a limited admin.

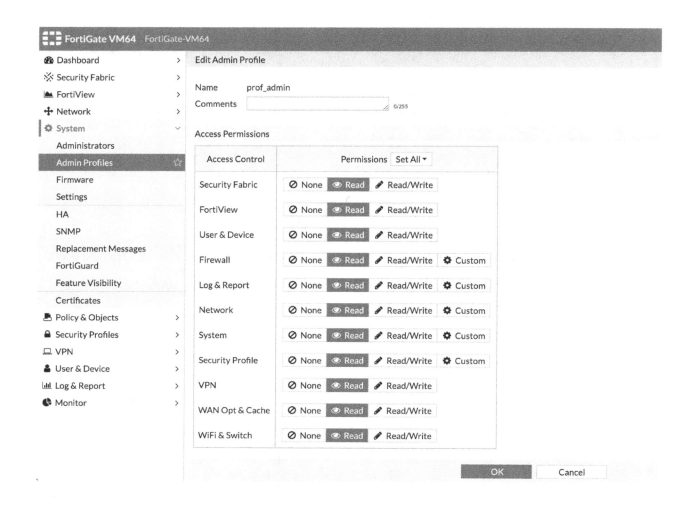

It has different **Read/Write** permissions, which we as Super admin can determine.

So let's create a new professional admin profile. Let's log out and enter again as the new professional admin and see the differences.

Our new administrator will be a local administrator

and the credentials will be stored in the FortiGate internal storage.

We are not using a remote server, we'll assign a very simple password just for the demo purposes.

On the right corner of your FortiGate interface, you will see the javascript CLI icon (arrow followed by an underscore), just click on it and the command line will open up

```
FortiGate-VM64 # config system admin

FortiGate-VM64 (admin) # edit ofershm

FortiGate-VM64 (ofershm) # set accprofile prof_admin

FortiGate-VM64 (ofershm) # set password 123456

FortiGate-VM64 (ofershm) #
```

The administrator we created has a **Professional admin** profile

Once configured, let's move over to the **admin menu** which is on the top right side of the interface, and log out.

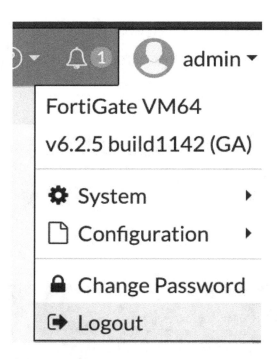

And let's log in again as the new professional admin I am using the **"ofershm"** username and the new password that we have just created.

Alright, it looks similar. But when we will move between the different menus. We will see that as a **professional admin** (which has only the read permissions) we cannot do anything. We can only view the current configuration. We cannot create or edit new interfaces or policies.

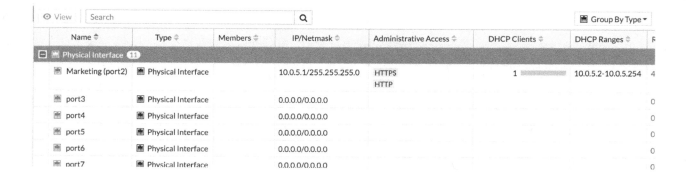

Super Admin **Account**

Now let's create another **admin**, this time a **super admin**

Again open up the **CLI**

Start by typing **"config system admin"** (no need for the quotes)

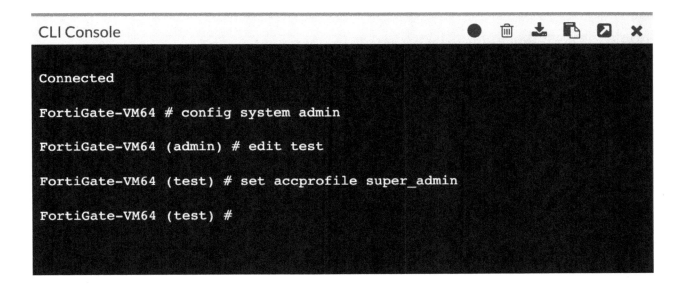

```
CLI Console                                    ●  🗑  ⬇  📋  ↗  ✕

Connected

FortiGate-VM64 # config system admin

FortiGate-VM64 (admin) # edit test

FortiGate-VM64 (test) # set accprofile super_admin

FortiGate-VM64 (test) #
```

The next thing to do is to name our admin, let's name it test admin. We do that using the edit command
"edit test"

A new entry was added. the **test** admin.
Now, the second thing to do is to set its profile. **Remember**, we have two main profiles. The first one is the **super admin**, which is the root admin , The second admin is the **professional admin** which is also used usually for specific tasks to

administrate another virtual domain in your FortiGate. So we'll use the **super admin**.

Continue by typing **" set accprofile super_admin"**, that will set us as a super admin

Now let's set a password for that admin, let's set a simple password (don't use that in real environments). And let's set a trusted host. **a trusted host** is a place from where the admin will connect to our FortiGate. A good practice is to set up a trusted host from within the subnets, or the IP address in our home in our admin's home, or from the work.

Alright, so now we have configured one trusted host, we can configure several trusted hosts.

```
CLI Console                                    ●  🗑  ⬇  📋  ↗  ✖

Connected

FortiGate-VM64 # config system admin

FortiGate-VM64 (admin) # edit test

FortiGate-VM64 (test) # set accprofile super_admin

FortiGate-VM64 (test) # set password 123456

FortiGate-VM64 (test) # set trusthost1 10.0.3.88█
```

Now we can set up more configurations such as the remote authentication, do you want to be authenticated using a remote server such as a radius or LDAP, or maybe do it locally on your FortiGate. This time, we will disable remote authentication, we can also set up a two-factor authentication which we will do next.

So this is the basic, the most basic admin profile configuration. Let's end it. And let's see it using our graphical user interface.

Name ⇕	Trusted Hosts ⇕	Profile ⇕	Type ⇕
⊟ System Administrator ③			
👤 admin		super_admin	Local
ofershm		prof_admin	Local
test	10.0.3.0/24	super_admin	Local

The next thing is something that is quite interesting. Now, you're a privileged admin. You're a **super admin**, and you have professional admins that administer different tasks in your FortiGate.

You can set up different things based on the fact that you're the privileged admin, such as password expiry for those professional admins.

How do you do it?
Type **"config system password policy"**
We can see that the status is currently enabled
If it is disabled, just enable it.

```
FortiGate-VM64 # config system password-policy

FortiGate-VM64 (password-policy) # show
config system password-policy
end

FortiGate-VM64 (password-policy) # set status enable

FortiGate-VM64 (password-policy) # show full-configuration
config system password-policy
    set status enable
    set apply-to admin-password
    set minimum-length 8
    set min-lower-case-letter 0
    set min-upper-case-letter 0
    set min-non-alphanumeric 0
    set min-number 0
    set change-4-characters disable
    set expire-status disable
    set reuse-password enable
end

FortiGate-VM64 (password-policy) # █
```

Using **MFA**

You can use **2-factor authentication**. such as a token with your administrator account.

You can use different Token solutions, but here we will look at one of the coolest methods, which is using our email

For the purpose of our demonstration, we will use my second admin account which is "test", it is a professional admin account. Now if I'll try to edit it using the GUI, we will see that indeed, two-factor authentication, we only have two possibilities. The first one is **FortiToken** and the second one is the **FortiToken Cloud.**

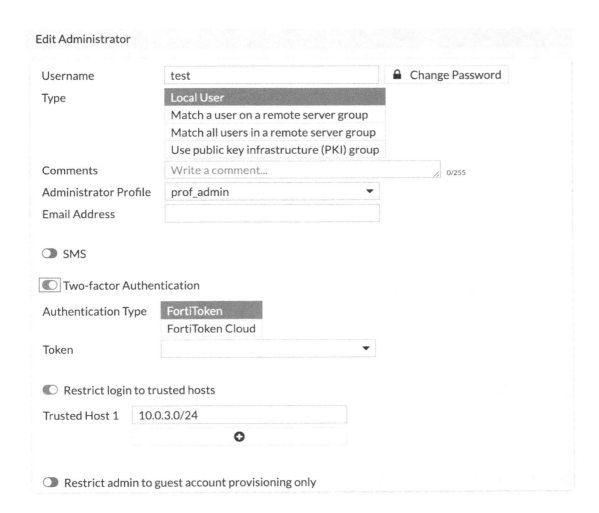

To get our third option, which is the email, we should open our command line and type **"config system admin"**

```
CLI Console                                    ● 🗑 ⤓ 📋 ⤢ ✖

Connected

FortiGate-VM64 # config system admin

FortiGate-VM64 (admin) # edit test

FortiGate-VM64 (test) # set two-factor email

FortiGate-VM64 (test) # set email-to orangehello@gmail.com

FortiGate-VM64 (test) # end
```

Now you will add the profile that you wish to add the email two-factor authentication In my case, it's **"test"**

You will set the two-factor email which enables you to have The third option on the GUI itself and you can set the email to where to send the token itself.

Let's set it to **orangehello@gmail.com**

"set two-factor email"
"set email-to orangehello@gmail.com"

let's end it.

Now if we will refresh the page, we will see that we have a third option

Edit Administrator

Username	test	🔒 Change Password
Type	**Local User**	
	Match a user on a remote server group	
	Match all users in a remote server group	
	Use public key infrastructure (PKI) group	
Comments	Write a comment...	0/255
Administrator Profile	prof_admin ▼	
Email Address	orangehello@gmail.com	

◯ SMS

◯ Two-factor Authentication

Authentication Type	FortiToken
	FortiToken Cloud
	Email based two-factor authentication

◯ Restrict login to trusted hosts

Trusted Host 1	10.0.3.0/24
	➕

◯ Restrict admin to guest account provisioning only

The next thing to do is to go to System Settings, set up your custom or default email service. I've left that using the Fortinet SMTP server, but you can use your own SMTP settings.

Email Service ⓘ

Use custom settings   ◯

SMTP Server	notification.fortinet.net
Port	465
Authentication	Disable
Security Mode	SMTPS
Default Reply To	

Debug Logs ⓘ

Debug logs   ⬇ Download

Configuration Backup

Backing up your configuration should become second nature. You can backup your configuration to a TFTP server, to your local disk, or to a USB drive

Let's start by looking at our current configuration using the CLI

"Show full-configuration"

```
Connected

FortiGate-VM64 # show full-configuration
#config-version=FGVM64-6.2.5-FW-build1142-200819:opmode=1:vdom=0:user=
#conf_file_ver=187814624930512
#buildno=1142
#global_vdom=1
config system global
    set admin-concurrent enable
    set admin-console-timeout 0
    set admin-https-pki-required disable
    set admin-https-ssl-versions tlsv1-1 tlsv1-2 tlsv1-3
    set admin-lockout-duration 60
    set admin-lockout-threshold 3
    set admin-login-max 100
    set admin-maintainer enable
    set admin-port 80
    set admin-restrict-local disable
    set admin-scp disable
    set admin-server-cert "self-sign"
    set admin-sport 443
    set admin-ssh-grace-time 120
    set admin-ssh-password enable
    set admin-ssh-port 22
    set admin-ssh-v1 disable
    set admin-telnet enable
    set admin-telnet-port 23
--More--              set admintimeout 5
--More--              set alias "FortiGate-VM64"
--More--              set allow-traffic-redirect enable
--More--              set anti-replay strict
--More--              set arp-max-entry 131072
--More--              set auth-cert "self-sign"
--More--              set auth-http-port 1000
--More--              set auth-https-port 1003
--More--              set auth-keepalive disable
--More--              set auth-session-limit block-new
--More--              set auto-auth-extension-device enable
--More--              set autorun-log-fsck disable
--More--              set av-affinity "0"
--More--
```

This command will list all the configurations that are currently on your FortiGate, including interfaces, policies, protocols, services, passwords, accounts …

To backup, your configuration, navigate to the top right page of your FortiGate admin page, where and click on the **admin** menu

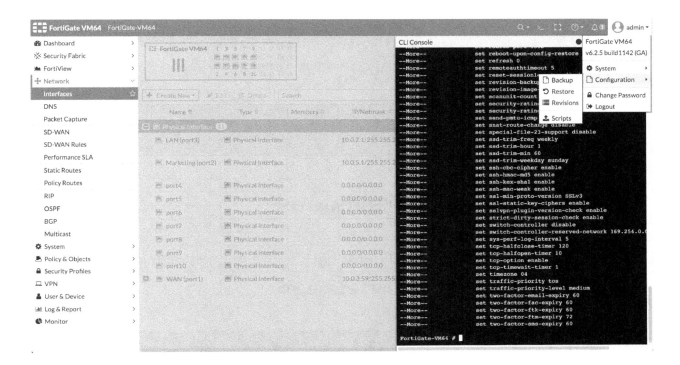

The menu will show up with several options (logout, change password, configuration)

Choose **configuration** and a new page will open up

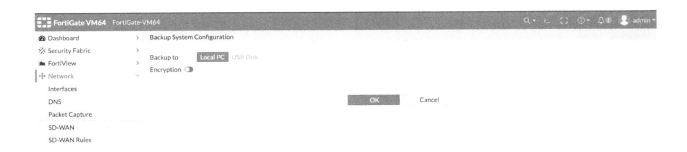

Here you will find the option, to backup your configuration to a local PC, or to a USB disk and to either encrypt the configuration file with a password or to keep it in plain Text

----

NOTE: EVEN IF YOU DECIDED TO KEEP THE CONFIGURATION WITH NO ENCRYPTION, YOUR PASSWORDS (ADMIN PASSWORD, USER PASSWORDS, WILL STILL BE HASHED, SO NO ONE CAN USE THEM)

Backup Restore and **Revisions**

To restore a configuration, you will move back to the top right admin menu
On the menu choose **Configuration --- Restore**

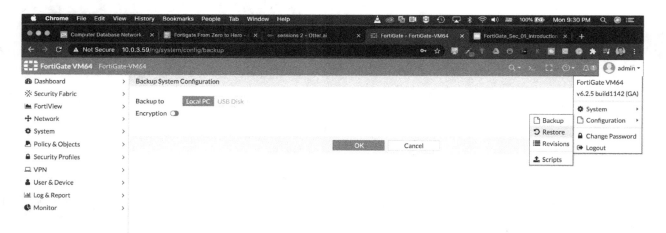

You can restore the configuration backup, to other FortiGate machines, but it depends
- If the back up wasn't encrypted, you will need a **similar FortiGate model**
- If the backup was encrypted, you will need the **password, similar model, and similar firmware**

Restore System Configuration

Restore from   **Local PC**   USB Disk

File   ⊕ Upload

Password   [_____] 👁

       OK   Cancel

A good practice is to save revisions of your backup with descriptions for each, so you will know what has changed

On the admin menu **configurations --- revisions - save changes**

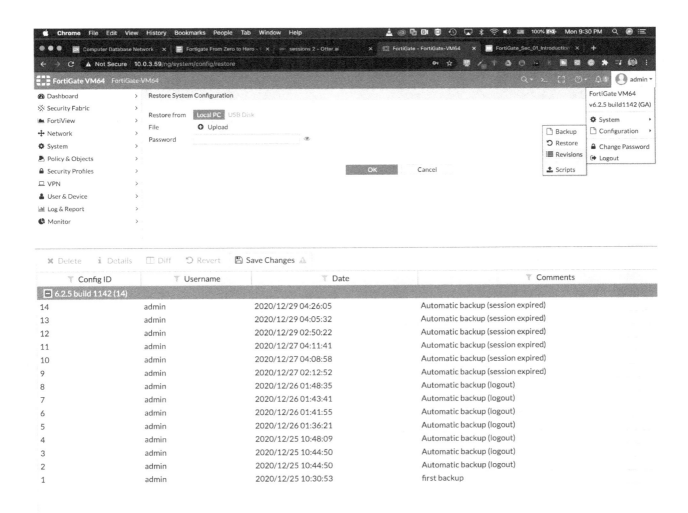

Automatic Backup on **LogOut**

One of the coolest features you can use is to automatically backup your configuration on every log-out.

Open your CLI and write the following:

```
CLI Console                                    ● 🗑 ⭳ 🗐 ⬀ ✖

Connected

FortiGate-VM64 # config system global

FortiGate-VM64 (global) # set revision-backup-on-logout enable

FortiGate-VM64 (global) # end
```

Now make changes to the configuration and logout

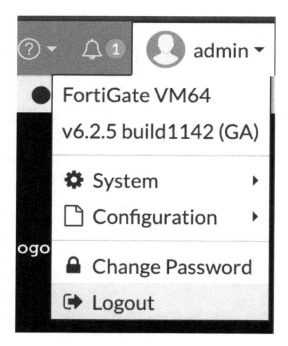

Now navigate again to revisions, and you will see a new automatic backup on logout message

Automatic backup (logout)
Automatic backup (logout)
Automatic backup (logout)
Automatic backup (logout)
Automatic backup (logout)
Automatic backup (logout)
Automatic backup (logout)
first backup

Backup to a TFTP server with an **Automation Stitch**

You can backup your configuration to a TFTP server, we will do it using a CLI Script and an Automation Stitch

Automation is fundamental to every security appliance out there and FortiGate is not different. you can use automation in different ways we will look at the most frequent use which is backing up

The idea behind **automation stitches** is simple. it is very similar to IFTTT (if this then that) you choose a **trigger** and you choose the **action** that will follow.

So let's create our new first stitch. Let's name it **"Backup"**.

Our trigger will be **"schedule"**, we will set a daily hour, in which a backup will happen automatically, using a CLI Script

So let's move to **security fabric--automation**

- Create a **new Automation Stitch**
- Name it **Backup**
- And on triggers choose **"schedule"**

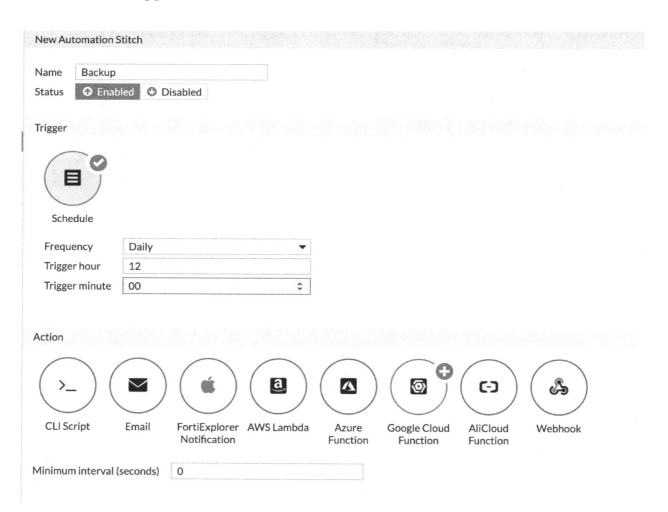

Here we have a scheduled event that will back up our device daily at 12 o'clock
The next thing to do is to set up an action using a CLI script that will trigger a
backup.

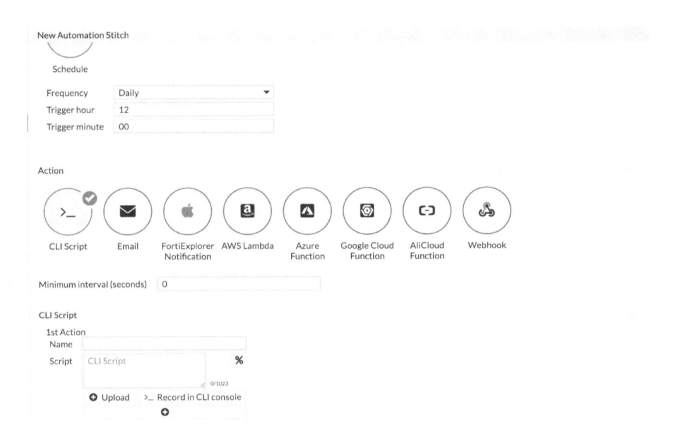

Our CLI script will be **"execute backup config tftp back.conf 10.0.7.22"**

- **Back.conf** = the name of the file
- **10.0.7.22** = the IP address of the TFTP server

CLI Script

1st Action

Name
> back

Script
> execute backup config tftp
> back.conf 10.0.7.22

%

46/1023

⊕ Upload   >_ Record in CLI console

⊕

The Idea Behind Automation Is That You Can Do A Bunch Of Things Using
The Automation Scripts That Will Help You To Offload Daily Tasks

---

Configuring a new LAN interface

You can configure your LAN interface using the graphical user interface, which is quite intuitive, or using the CLI as we did at the beginning, so here is a reminder and let's start from the basics

Configuring Interface with the **Command Line**

Start with **"Config system interface"**

Decide which port you want to configure the interface **"Edit port5"**

How will it get it's IP address, static or by DHCP **"Set mode static/DHCP"**

NOTE - Using The Tab Key, You Can Toggle Between Different Options As In "DHCP" Vs "Static", You Can Also Use Tab To Auto-complete Commands

----

```
FortiGate-VM64 # FortiGate-VM64 # config system interface

FortiGate-VM64 (interface) # edit port5

FortiGate-VM64 (port5) # set mode static
```

The second thing to do is set the protocols allowed to access that interface. you do that using the **"set allowaccess"**

```
CLI Console                                        ● 🗑 ⬇ 📋 ↗ ✕

FortiGate-VM64 # FortiGate-VM64 # config system interface

FortiGate-VM64 (interface) # edit port5

FortiGate-VM64 (port5) # set mode static

FortiGate-VM64 (port5) # set ip 10.0.9.1/24

FortiGate-VM64 (port5) # set allowaccess http ping
```

This is the basic setup, but you can add up more information, actually a lot more information as seen in the screenshot

```
CLI Console                                        ● 🗑 ⬇ 📋 ↗ ✕

FortiGate-VM64 # FortiGate-VM64 # config system interface

FortiGate-VM64 (interface) # edit port5

FortiGate-VM64 (port5) # set mode static

FortiGate-VM64 (port5) # set ip 10.0.9.1/24

FortiGate-VM64 (port5) # set allowaccess http ping

FortiGate-VM64 (port5) # set macaddr 00:ff:ee:2e:3d:11

FortiGate-VM64 (port5) # set vdom root

FortiGate-VM64 (port5) # set status up

FortiGate-VM64 (port5) # set weight 200

FortiGate-VM64 (port5) # set type physical

FortiGate-VM64 (port5) # set src-check enable

FortiGate-VM64 (port5) # set explicit-web-proxy enable

FortiGate-VM64 (port5) #
```

Configuring interfaces is one of those things that determines and changes your topology and network capabilities completely. If you want to see which capabilities and support can be added, just type :

"config system interface"

"edit port (X)"

"show full-configuration "

```
FortiGate-VM64 (port1) # show full-configuration
config system interface
    edit "port1"
        set vdom "root"
        set vrf 0
        set fortilink disable
        set mode static
        set dhcp-relay-service disable
        set ip 10.0.3.59 255.255.255.0
        set allowaccess https http
        set fail-detect disable
        set pptp-client disable
        set arpforward enable
        set broadcast-forward disable
        set bfd global
        set l2forward disable
        set icmp-send-redirect enable
        set icmp-accept-redirect enable
        set vlanforward disable
        set stpforward disable
        set ips-sniffer-mode disable
        set ident-accept disable
        set ipmac disable
        set subst disable
        set substitute-dst-mac 00:00:00:00:00:00
--More--                      set status up
--More--                      set netbios-forward disable
--More--                      set wins-ip 0.0.0.0
--More--                      set type physical
--More--                      set ring-rx 0
--More--                      set ring-tx 0
--More--                      set netflow-sampler disable
--More--                      set sflow-sampler disable
--More--                      set src-check enable
```

Configuring Interface **Using the GUI**

Let's assume that:

- Our FortiGate management interface is at port 3 with the 10.0.5.1 address
- Our FortiGate is connected to an ISP router, through port 1, it will be our WAN interface
- Our new LAN will be at **port 10**, at the **10.0.7.0** subnet
- Anyone Who is connected to port 10, will be part of that LAN and will get an IP address from its an internal DHCP server that we will set

Name ⇕	Type ⇕	Members ⇕	IP/Netmask ⇕	Administrative Access ⇕
⊟ 📶 **Physical Interface** (10)				
📶 LAN (port10)	📶 Physical Interface		10.0.7.1/255.255.255.0	HTTPS SSH
📶 management (port3)	📶 Physical Interface		10.0.5.1/255.255.255.0	HTTPS SSH HTTP
📶 port2	📶 Physical Interface		0.0.0.0/0.0.0.0	
📶 port4	📶 Physical Interface		0.0.0.0/0.0.0.0	
📶 port5	📶 Physical Interface		0.0.0.0/0.0.0.0	
📶 port6	📶 Physical Interface		0.0.0.0/0.0.0.0	
📶 port7	📶 Physical Interface		0.0.0.0/0.0.0.0	
📶 port8	📶 Physical Interface		0.0.0.0/0.0.0.0	
📶 port9	📶 Physical Interface		0.0.0.0/0.0.0.0	
📶 WAN (port1)	📶 Physical Interface		10.0.3.55/255.255.255.0	HTTPS HTTP

Configure Your **LAN**

Click on **network--- interface---edit** (Choose any interface ,in our case it is port 10), you will enter the interface configuration page

Name your interface using the **Alias** field (very important)
The second thing is the role, you have 4 options:

- LAN
- WAN
- DMZ
- Undefined

We will choose **LAN**

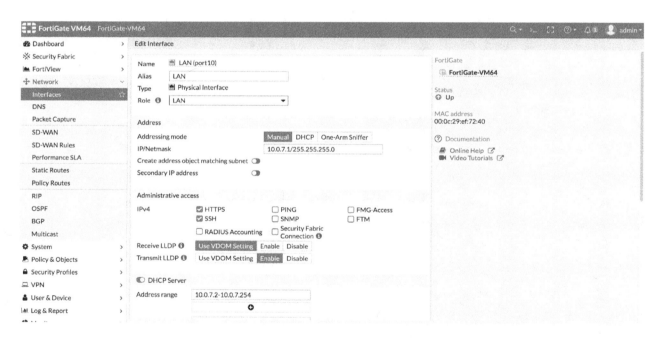

At the address field, choose your LAN gateway IP address, you can choose to get one from a DHCP server, but will set it in a static (manual) way

From here, you can configure the **administrative access** that will allow you to connect to that interface, either **HTTPS, SSH** …

Address

Addressing mode   [Manual]   DHCP   One-Arm Sniffer

IP/Netmask   10.0.7.1/255.255.255.0

Secondary IP address ⬤

Administrative access

IPv4   ☑ HTTPS   ☐ PING   ☐ FMG-Access

                    ☑ SSH   ☐ SNMP   ☐ FTM

                    ☐ RADIUS Accounting   ☐ Security Fabric Connection ⓘ

Note — there are tons of things that you configure on your interface, but we will focus on the most basic and fundamental

----

Your LAN will lease IP addresses to all members of the subnet, so we will set a **DHCP server**, by enabling it

DHCP **service**

You can control the number of IP addresses, bare in mind, that you don't necessarily need to have 254 addresses available, if your LAN has only 15 employees, use 30 or 40 addresses

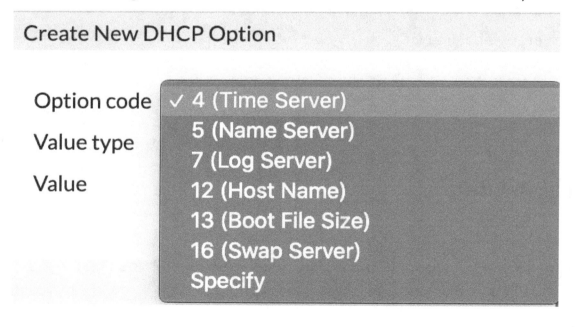

DHCP Server

Address range	10.0.7.2-10.0.7.35
	⊕
Netmask	255.255.255.0
Default gateway	Same as Interface IP Specify
DNS server	Same as System DNS Same as Interface IP Specify
Lease time ⓘ ◉	604800 second(s)
⊕ Advanced	

If you enable the advanced options, you will have more options, as using a **DHCP relay**, that is if you don't want to use your interface DHCP server, you can also configure, additional **DHCP options, known as scopes** (as in the case, where you will want to send your wireless clients the IP address of their a Wi-Fi controller, change the Lease time or send an NTP server address)

Create New DHCP Option

Option code	✓ 4 (Time Server)
Value type	5 (Name Server)
Value	7 (Log Server)
	12 (Host Name)
	13 (Boot File Size)
	16 (Swap Server)
	Specify

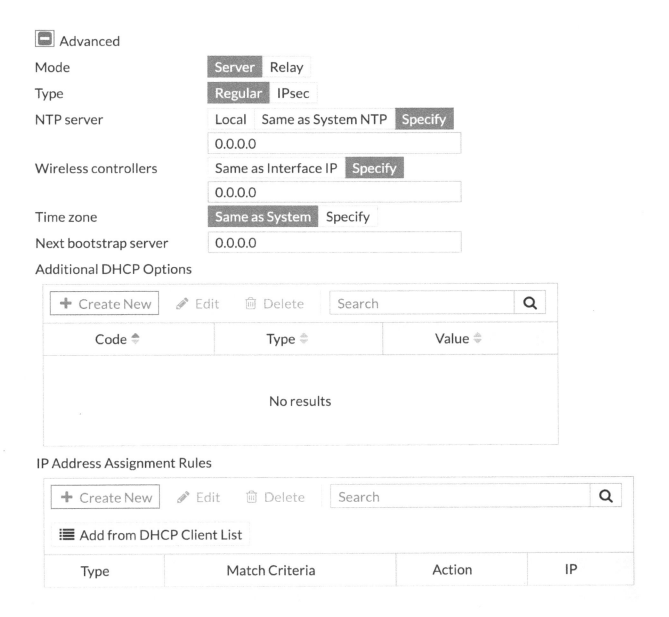

DHCP configuration also includes the ability to assign or reserve **IP** addresses to specific MAC address, or to block **MAC** addresses from getting IP addresses

MAC reservation **access control**

If you already have clients that are connected to our interface, you can choose to Add them from the DHCP client list , to the list of MAC addresses that you wish to assign different rules on them .

☰ Add from DHCP Client List			
Type	Match Criteria	Action	IP
Implicit	Unknown MAC Addresses	Assign IP	

For **unknown MAC addresses**, we can decide either to assign IP or to block them from getting any IP address from our DHCP server.

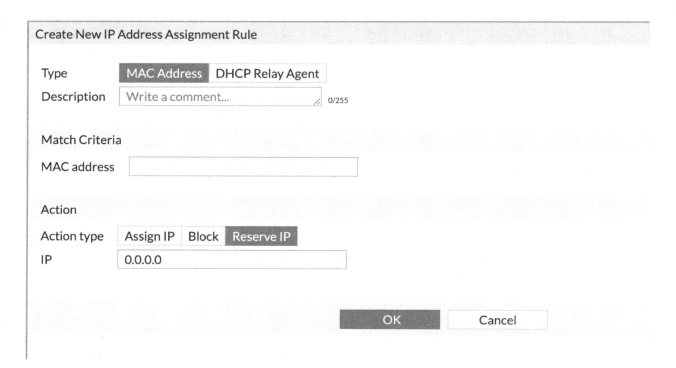

In IP address assignment rule create **New**

And In the **action** type, you can choose between

- **Assign IP**- Bind a specific IP to a MAC address

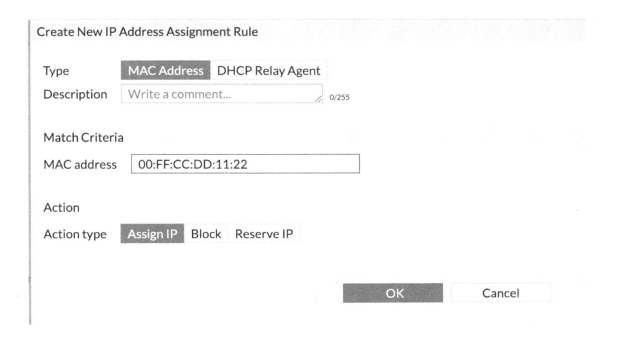

- **Block**-The MAC address will not get any IP Address

- **Reserve IP** - Permits the DHCP to assign an IP address from its pool. The receiving device will always get the same address

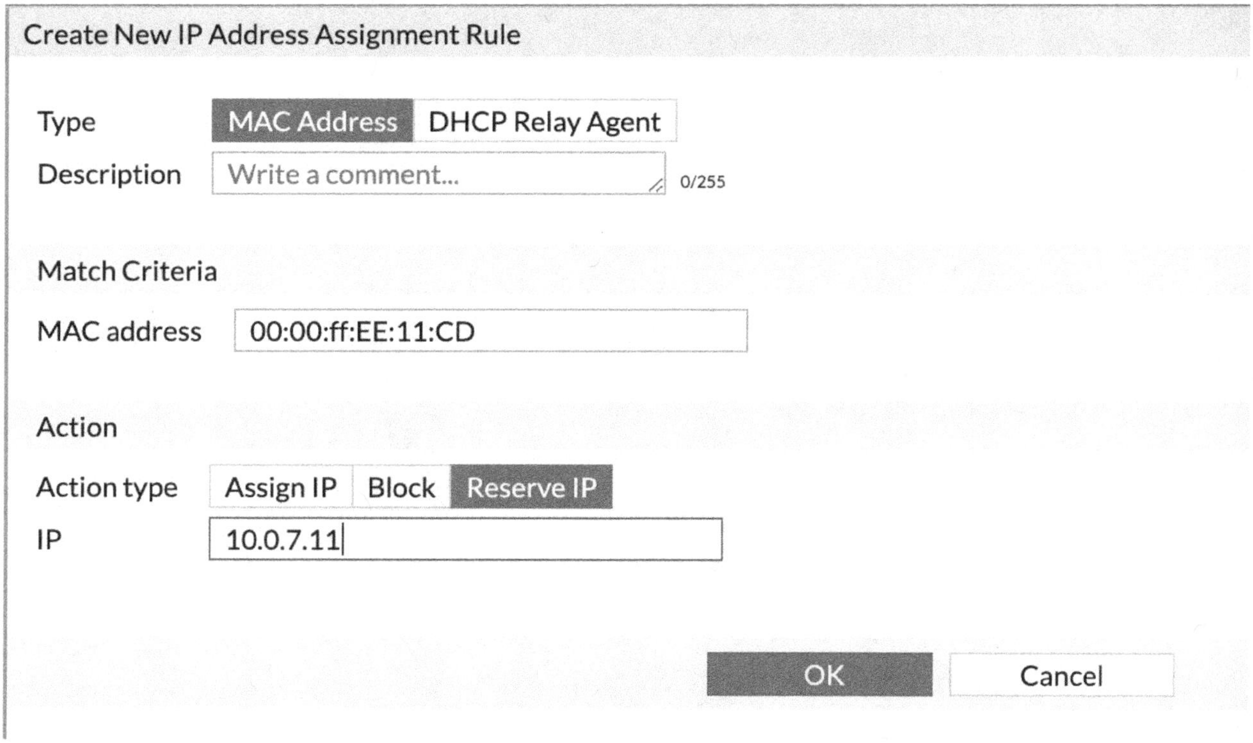

Create New IP Address Assignment Rule

Type   [MAC Address]   DHCP Relay Agent

Description   [Write a comment...   ]   0/255

Match Criteria

MAC address   [00:00:ff:EE:11:CD]

Action

Action type   [Assign IP | Block | **Reserve IP**]

IP   [10.0.7.11]

[**OK**]   [Cancel]

-

Following our Basic **DHCP server** Configuration, we can enable several more features, one of them is **device detection** (very useful when you have different types of devices and operating systems in your network) and enable a **captive portal** authentication for the employees or a specific group of employees (good for outsourcing employees)

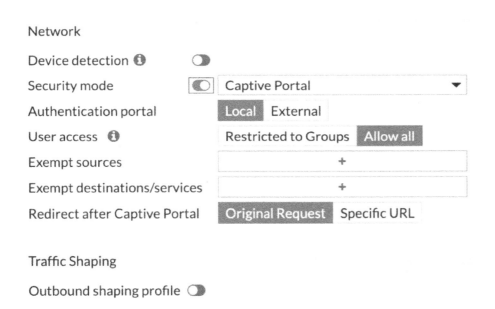

Captive Portal

Captive Portals are a common security procedure, used consistently on our networks for guests or even when outsource employees work within your internal LAN, connecting through ethernet wall sockets.

One way to do so is to enforce it by creating a **VLAN** (virtual LAN) on your subnet interface, apply a captive portal on that interface, and create an outsource employed group

In our current topology, We will not use LDAP For our outsource group (although it better to do so and more reasonable, but let's make things simpler) we will use our local FortiGate firewall database

Our Topology

Quite a simple Topology, SMB switch connected to our Marketing LAN, and a FortiGate that is connected to the ISP router

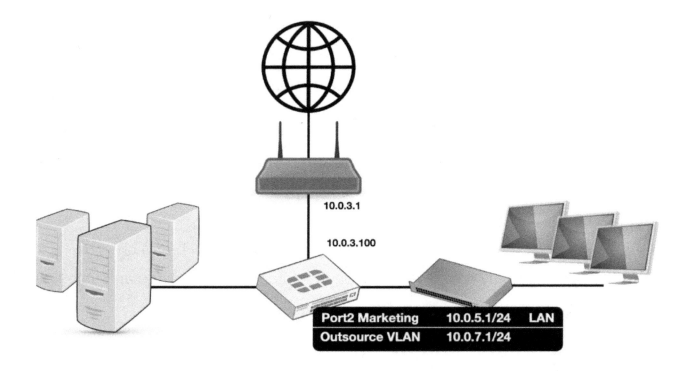

Port2 Marketing 10.0.5.1/24 LAN
Outsource VLAN 10.0.7.1/24

On your FortiGate admin page, choose **network —interfaces**

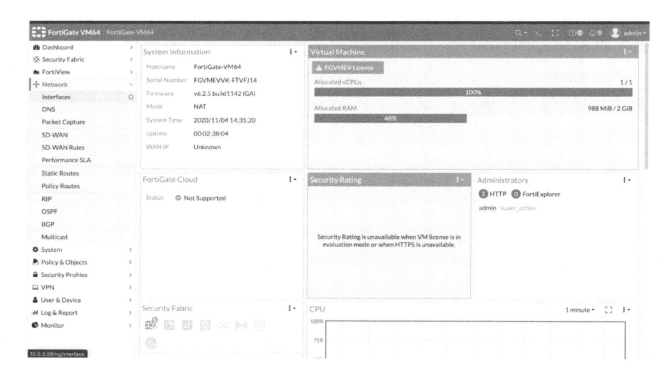

The opened screen will list all Interfaces on your Fortigate firewall, we will choose to apply our captive portal to our **Marketing LAN**, but you can choose to do it, on any LAN you wish

Our **Marketing LAN** has Connected to **Port 2** and the subnet is **10.0.5.0/24**

Employees on that LAN are connected through the switch which is connected To the Fortigate Firewall, Currently with No VLAN"s

VLAN **Creation**

Let's create the **VLAN** that will be used to connect our outsource employees to the network

VLANs are one of the most fundamental concepts in networking. So you have your LAN, this is your broadcast domain. Now you're limited with physical interfaces and you want to create more broadcast domains for other appliances, other users, how do you do it? Using VLANs?

You can create VLANs using the GUI, the graphical user interface by moving to create a new interface, and VLAN.

So move to the create a new interface, on our network interface page, and **Choose an interface**

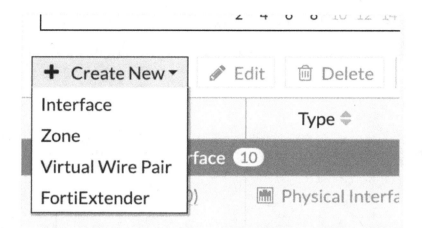

The New Page that will be opened will allow you to create new interfaces (**Software switch, Loopback, SSID**…) we will focus on our VLAN Interface, which will allow us to create another **broadcast domain** running on our physical **port 2**

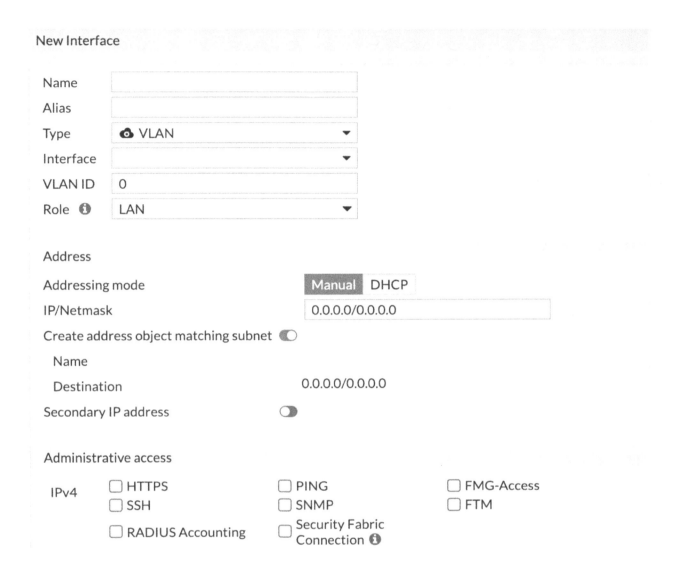

Now, Let's configure our new VLAN

- **Name:** outsource
- **Alias:** let's give it the same number as our Vlan ID which will be 100
- **Type:** we will choose Vlan out of all choices
- **Interface:** here we choose the physical interface that will occupy our VLAN, in our case it is Marketing port 2
- **VLAN ID:** that's the 802.1q tagging of our VLAN as seen by the switch
- **Role:** we will choose LAN, as it will be used as a local area network for our outsource employees

Name	outsource
Alias	100
Type	☁ VLAN ▼
Interface	🖥 Marketing (port2) ▼
VLAN ID	100
Role ⓘ	LAN ▼

REMEMBER our VLAN, is another Local area network of itself

Now let's assign a new IP address at the 10.0.7.0 subnet, a DHCP service, so our employees will lease IP's and administrative access for the admin using HTTPS and SSH

New Interface

Name	outsource
Alias	100
Type	☁ VLAN ▼
Interface	🏢 Marketing (port2) ▼
VLAN ID	100
Role ⓘ	LAN ▼

Address

Addressing mode   [Manual] DHCP

IP/Netmask   10.0.7.1/24

Create address object matching subnet ⬤

   Name   🗒 outsource address

   Destination   10.0.7.1/24

Secondary IP address ⬤

Administrative access

IPv4

☑ HTTPS   ☑ PING   ☐ FMG-Access
☑ SSH   ☐ SNMP   ☐ FTM
☐ RADIUS Accounting   ☐ Security Fabric Connection ⓘ

⬤ DHCP Server

Address range   10.0.7.2-10.0.7.254

Let's click **OK** for now, we will get back to our VLAN interface again.

On the interface page, you will see the **+ sign** next to our marketing interface

➕ 🏢 Marketing (port2)	🏢 Physical Interface	10.0.5.1/255.255.255.0	HTTPS SSH

Click on the **+ sign**, and you will see our new outsource **VLAN 100** at the

10.0.7.1

⊟	🗠 Marketing (port2)	🗠 Physical Interface	10.0.5.1/255.255.255.0	HTTPS SSH
⌙•➔	☁ 100 (outsource)	☁ VLAN	10.0.7.1/255.255.255.0	PING HTTPS SSH

User **Group**

Now let's create a group for our outsource employees, as said, we will not use LDAP or any other remote authentication servers, we will use our local firewall database

Move over to **User & Device — User Definition**

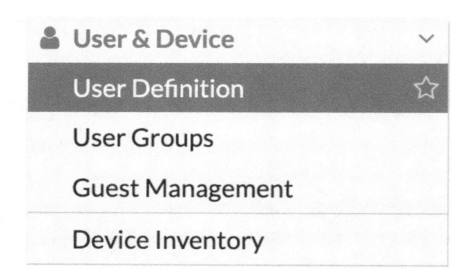

Here you will create your outsource employees, let's create two employees
Click New

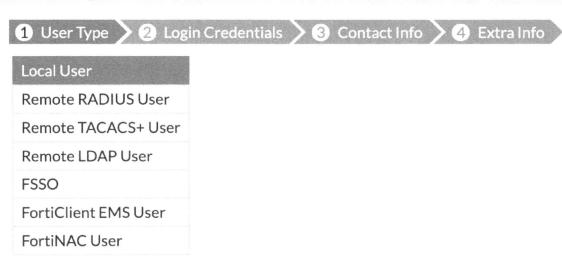

Coose Local User and click **Next**

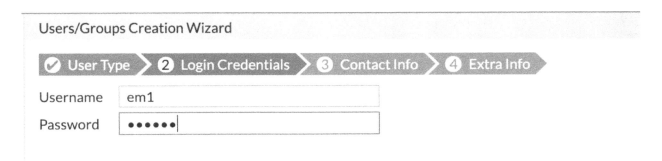

Choose a **Username and Password**, that will be used when your employees, will authenticate, through the captive portal

Click **Next**, you will have the option to add an email and two-factor authentication using tokens, lets just add an **email**

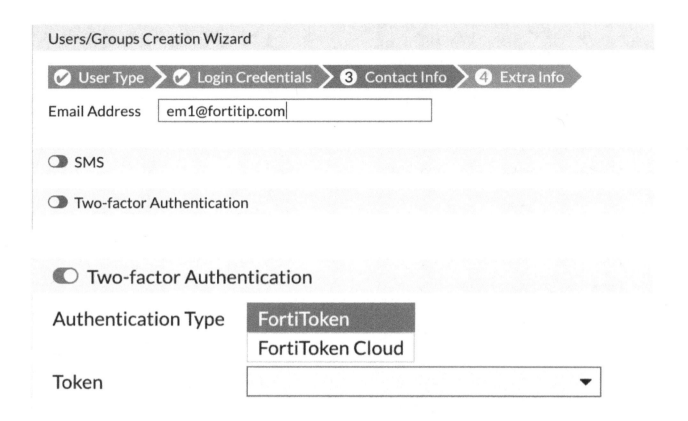

Click **submit** on the next page, we will assign this employee to a dedicated group soon

Create as many users as you need, in the end, you will see, them on the user's page

Now let's assign the new Users to a dedicated group, this group will be used in

Our captive portal. click **User Group ---- create new**

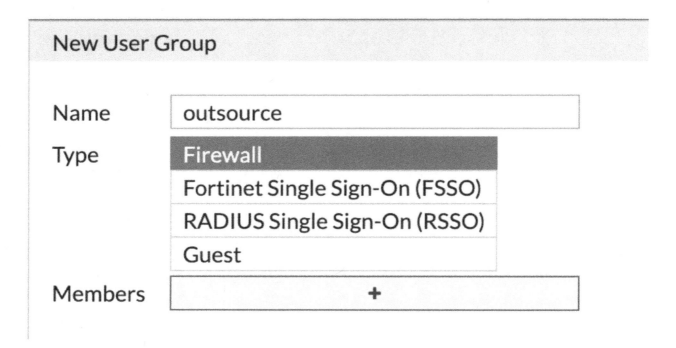

Name your group and click on the **Members + sign**, here you will add the new users that you created

Click OK, The new group was created

Guest-group   ▦ Firewall   👤 ofer

SSO_Guest_Users   👥 Fortinet Single Sign-On (FSSO)

outsource   ▦ Firewall   👤 em1
      👤 ofer

Now let's get back to our interface page, choose the **VLAN**, We have created, and click **edit**

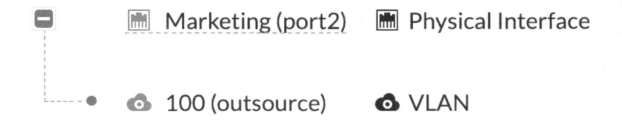

🖧 Marketing (port2)   🖧 Physical Interface

☁ 100 (outsource)   ☁ VLAN

Scroll down to the network part, where you will see the **Security mode** button,

and **enable** it

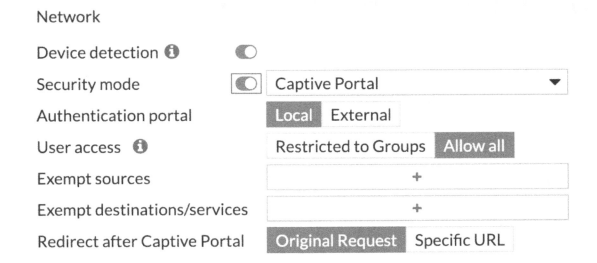

Network

Device detection ℹ️   ⬤◯

Security mode   ◯⬤   Captive Portal ▼

Authentication portal   Local   External

User access ℹ️   Restricted to Groups   Allow all

Exempt sources   ➕

Exempt destinations/services   ➕

Redirect after Captive Portal   Original Request   Specific URL

Choose **Authentication portal — Local** (if you choose External, it will ask you to refer to an external server

User access — choose restricted to groups

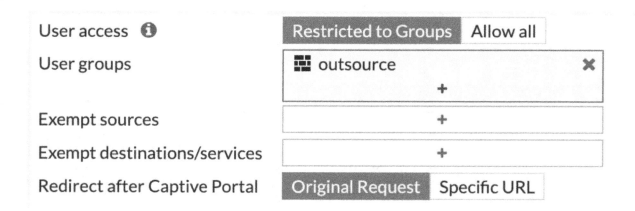

Now let's choose our user group, click on the **+ sign** next to **User groups** and choose the group, that you have just created

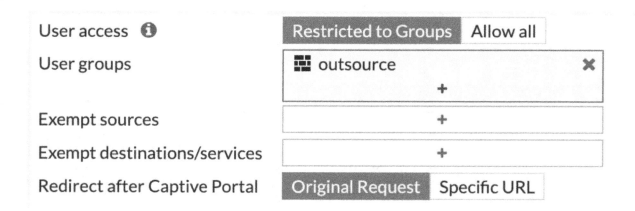

You can also exempt sources, that you do not want to be directed to the captive portal page. you will need to create a **firewall address object**, as shown in the next chapter

Press OK. that's it, you have created your first captive portal

You will need to make sure, that your switch supports Vlan's, and to assign the relevant **VLAN100** on that switch also, besides that, you're done, your FortiGate port2, has become a Trunk port, that can except **native VLAN traffic**, and your outsource VLAN 100 traffic

Creating VLAN in **The CLI**

We can also create Vlan's Using the CLI, so let's do that to our marketing interface at the 10.0.5.0/24 subnet, assuming that we need another broadcast domain for outsource employees

Our VLAN ID will be 100, and it will be associated with port 2, which is our Marketing Port and it's IP address will be 10.0.2.1

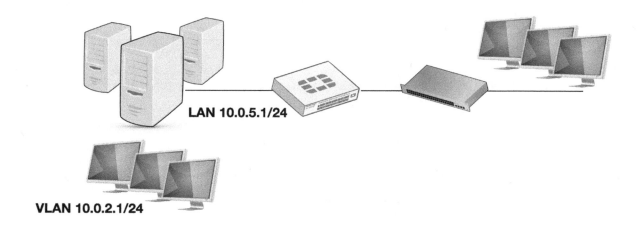

LAN 10.0.5.1/24

VLAN 10.0.2.1/24

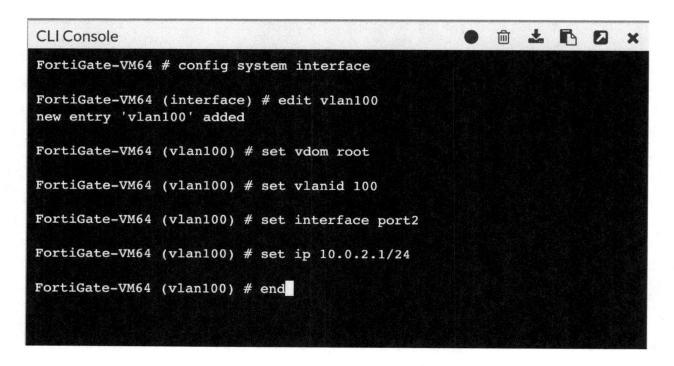

```
CLI Console                                    ● 🗑 ⬇ 📋 ↗ ✖

FortiGate-VM64 # config system interface

FortiGate-VM64 (interface) # edit vlan100
new entry 'vlan100' added

FortiGate-VM64 (vlan100) # set vdom root

FortiGate-VM64 (vlan100) # set vlanid 100

FortiGate-VM64 (vlan100) # set interface port2

FortiGate-VM64 (vlan100) # set ip 10.0.2.1/24

FortiGate-VM64 (vlan100) # end
```

And now if we move back to our **interfaces page** , we can see that we have a
new VLAN interface

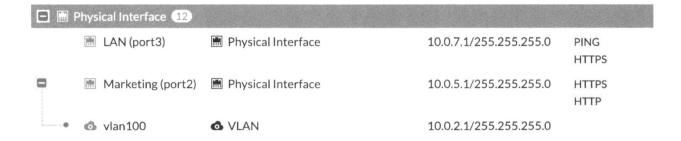

⊟ 🏢 **Physical Interface** 12				
🏢 LAN (port3)	🏢 Physical Interface	10.0.7.1/255.255.255.0	PING HTTPS
⊟ 🏢 Marketing (port2)	🏢 Physical Interface	10.0.5.1/255.255.255.0	HTTPS HTTP
⬤ ☁ vlan100	☁ VLAN	10.0.2.1/255.255.255.0	

Our new VLAN behaves just like any other local area network, you can keep on configuring DHCP services, DNS services, just about anything on that VLAN the same way as you were doing on any other interface.

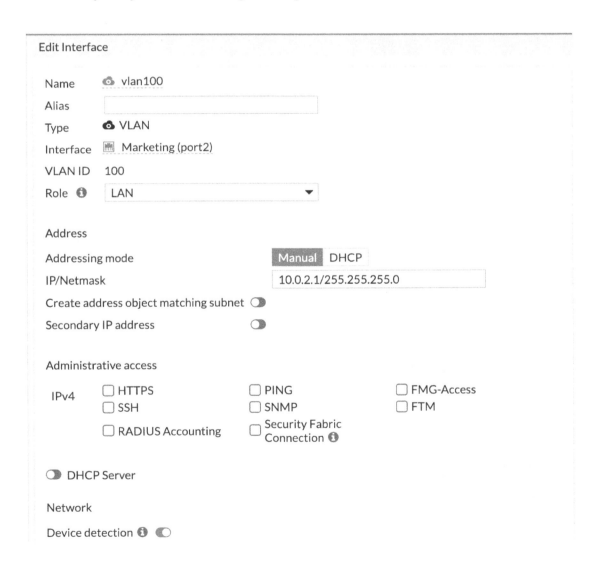

Edit Interface

Name ☁ vlan100
Alias [   ]
Type ☁ VLAN
Interface 🏢 Marketing (port2)
VLAN ID 100
Role ⓘ [LAN   ▼]

Address

Addressing mode [Manual] DHCP
IP/Netmask [10.0.2.1/255.255.255.0   ]
Create address object matching subnet ◯
Secondary IP address ◯

Administrative access

IPv4 ☐ HTTPS   ☐ PING   ☐ FMG-Access
      ☐ SSH   ☐ SNMP   ☐ FTM
      ☐ RADIUS Accounting   ☐ Security Fabric Connection ⓘ

◯ DHCP Server

Network

Device detection ⓘ ◯

Creating firewall Address Objects

Your firewall rules will require you to recognize specific devices in your LAN, using IP address, Geographic location (in the case that we will want to block geo- address as destinations) and more.

So if for example, we have in our LAN a device, such as a **NAS** (network-attached storage) that we will want to open specific rules, only for him, it would be much more convenient to use an **Address Object**

To configure our address object in our LAN, we will use the command line, remember that:

- Our NAS belongs to the 10.0.7.0/24 subnet
- It is connected through port 10
- It has the 10.0.7.11 address

To get into the command line, click again on the **CLI symbol** at the top right side of the page which will open the command line

From here we will type the following

```
CLI Console                                    ● 🗑 ⬇ 📋 ↗ ✖

FortiGate-VM64 # config firewall address

FortiGate-VM64 (address) # edit "NAS"
new entry 'NAS' added

FortiGate-VM64 (NAS) # set associated-interface "port10"

FortiGate-VM64 (NAS) # set subnet 10.0.7.11 255.255.255.255

FortiGate-VM64 (NAS) #
```

- We have created a new object using the " **config firewall address** " command
- Named it "NAS" with "edit NAS"
- Associate it with the relevant interface (port 10) - **"set associated-interface port10"**
- And assigned an IP address - **"set subnet 10.0.7.11 255.255.255.255"**

Now we can use our address object in different policy scenarios to block or allow this specific object.

We can also create address objects using the GUI. just navigate to **Policy & Objects --- Addresses**

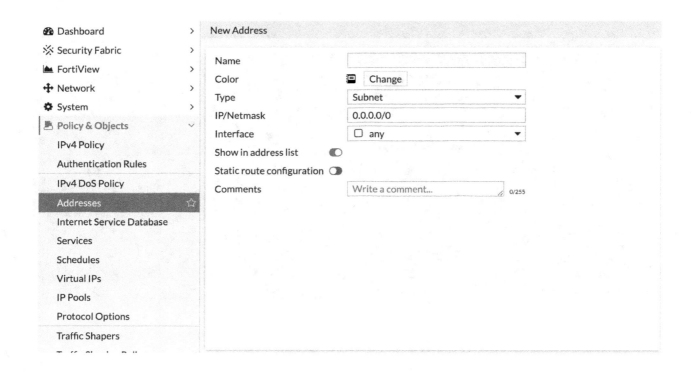

But this time let's configure another type of address object, the **GEO location** object. fill in the name, type of object, country, and interface

Click **OK**, you can see the address object in the list of addresses

all	Subnet	0.0.0.0/0
gmail.com	FQDN	gmail.com
iran	Geography	Iran, Islamic Republic of
login.microsoft.com	FQDN	login.microsoft.com
login.microsoftonline.com	FQDN	login.microsoftonline.com
login.windows.net	FQDN	login.windows.net

Summary

We started with an administrator set up, interface configuration with DHCP service running that will lease IP addresses to your clients, we have also configured a basic captive portal for a user group and finally, we have configured a firewall address object for a specific device on our subnet

We needed to create a firewall address object so that we could, later on, point specifically to that device on our subnet

Now it is time to let traffic from our interface get out to the internet with the static route and our first policy

Layer 3 Routing

Routing is a destination decision making in other words, it is the thing that controls how packets are sent along the path from source to destination. Routing is an OSI layer 3 decision, and network devices that belong to that class are known as Routers. Your FortiGate firewall is not only a next-generation firewall, but it is also a router

Network devices that perform routing, contain a **Routing Table**, which helps them to specify the next hop for a packet, using rules. your FortiGate does routing lookups every time it needs to route packets

Routing **Decisions**

FortiGate is a session aware firewall. When it receives a packet from a client towards any destination, it looks in the routing table, does a route lookup, and saves the routing information in this session table.

When it receives the **second packet**, the one that came from the destination towards the client, it saves the route lookup, it does another route lookup, it saves it into the session table.

Your FortiGate actually relies on three routing databases to forward the packets:

- The first one is the policy-based route
- The second one is the routing cache

- The third one is the FIB, the **Forwarding Information Base**. So let's take a look and see what is in each database.

When you check your routing table using the:

"get router info routing-table all"

```
FortiGate-VM64 # get router info routing-table all

Routing table for VRF=0
Codes: K - kernel, C - connected, S - static, R - RIP, B - BGP
       O - OSPF, IA - OSPF inter area
       N1 - OSPF NSSA external type 1, N2 - OSPF NSSA external type 2
       E1 - OSPF external type 1, E2 - OSPF external type 2
       i - IS-IS, L1 - IS-IS level-1, L2 - IS-IS level-2, ia - IS-IS inter
       * - candidate default

S*      0.0.0.0/0 [10/0] via 10.0.3.1, port1
C       10.0.3.0/24 is directly connected, port1
C       10.0.5.0/24 is directly connected, port2
C       10.0.7.0/24 is directly connected, port3


FortiGate-VM64 #
```

You will see the connected routes, you see the static routes, dynamic routes, such as OSPF or RIP, any route that is an active route

An active route is the best route to specific destinations on your FortiGate. If you use the same command with the database

"get router info routing-table database"

```
FortiGate-VM64 # get router info routing-table database

Routing table for VRF=0
Codes: K - kernel, C - connected, S - static, R - RIP, B - BGP
       O - OSPF, IA - OSPF inter area
       N1 - OSPF NSSA external type 1, N2 - OSPF NSSA external type 2
       E1 - OSPF external type 1, E2 - OSPF external type 2
       i - IS-IS, L1 - IS-IS level-1, L2 - IS-IS level-2, ia - IS-IS inte
       > - selected route, * - FIB route, p - stale info


S        0.0.0.0/0 [20/0] via 10.0.7.13, port3
S     *> 0.0.0.0/0 [10/0] via 10.0.3.1, port1
C     *> 10.0.3.0/24 is directly connected, port1
C     *> 10.0.5.0/24 is directly connected, port2
C     *> 10.0.7.0/24 is directly connected, port3


FortiGate-VM64 # █
```

You see every route that there is in the routing table, including routes that are not Active, as the route to 10.0.7.13.

One thing that you're not seeing on the routing table is the **Policy-Based routes**. If you move to network policy routes, you can actually create routes that are much more granular in terms of the protocol that is being used, the source address that is being used, and so on.

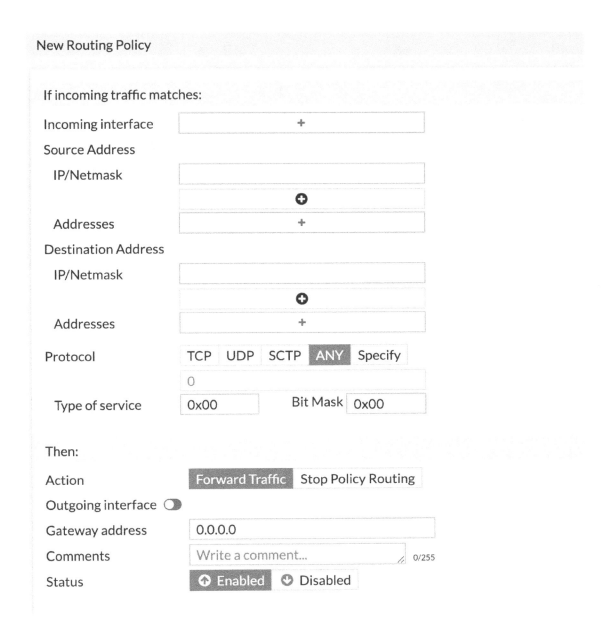

New Routing Policy

If incoming traffic matches:

Incoming interface   +

Source Address

  IP/Netmask

                    ➕

  Addresses   +

Destination Address

  IP/Netmask

                    ➕

  Addresses   +

Protocol   TCP UDP SCTP ANY Specify

            0

Type of service   0x00   Bit Mask 0x00

Then:

Action   Forward Traffic   Stop Policy Routing

Outgoing interface ⬤

Gateway address   0.0.0.0

Comments   Write a comment...   0/255

Status   ⬆ Enabled   ⬇ Disabled

Policy-Based **Routes**

Policy-based Routes can only be seen using the CLI, by typing:

"diag firewall proute list"

```
CLI Console                                    ● 🗑 ⬇ 📋 ↗ ✖

FortiGate-VM64 # diag firewall proute list
list route policy info(vf=root):

id=2113929219 static_route=3 dscp_tag=0xff 0xff flags=0x0 tos=0x00 tos_ma
source wildcard(1): 0.0.0.0/0.0.0.0
destination wildcard(1): 0.0.0.0/0.0.0.0
internet service(1): Netflix-Web(786433)
hit_count=0 last_used=2021-01-05 02:42:44

FortiGate-VM64 # ▊
```

Here you can see that I have a policy route with **Netflix** as the destination

The **Policy-Based Routes** are actually the first place that your FortiGate checks
to see if there's a route towards the destination that is in the policy-based route. If
it doesn't find a match, the second place that it goes to is the **routing cache**.

Routing **Cache**

The **Routing Cache** is actually a mechanism that deals with performance. you
want to route as fast as possible. And your FortiGate has a dedicated memory to
cache entries, that is, the routing cash, how can you see the routing cache?

"diag ip rtcache list"

```
FortiGate-VM64 # diag ip rtcache list

family=02 tab=254 vrf=0 vf=0 type=01 tos=0 flag=00000200
10.0.3.59@0->10.0.3.22@3(port1) gwy=0.0.0.0 prefsrc=0.0.0.0
ci: ref=2 lastused=16 expire=0 err=00000000 used=111 br=0 pmtu=1500

family=02 tab=254 vrf=0 vf=0 type=03 tos=0 flag=94000200
10.0.3.154@3(port1)->10.0.3.255@13(root) gwy=0.0.0.0 prefsrc=10.0.3.59
ci: ref=0 lastused=8 expire=0 err=00000000 used=29 br=0 pmtu=16436

family=02 tab=254 vrf=0 vf=0 type=01 tos=0 flag=00000200
0.0.0.0@0->208.91.112.53@3(port1) gwy=10.0.3.1 prefsrc=10.0.3.59
ci: ref=0 lastused=0 expire=0 err=00000000 used=12 br=0 pmtu=1500

family=02 tab=254 vrf=0 vf=0 type=01 tos=0 flag=04000200
10.0.5.7@4(port2)->188.172.246.170@3(port1) gwy=10.0.3.1 prefsrc=10.0.5.
ci: ref=1 lastused=24 expire=0 err=00000000 used=0 br=0 pmtu=1500

family=02 tab=254 vrf=0 vf=0 type=01 tos=0 flag=00000200
8.8.8.8@3(port1)->10.0.5.7@4(port2) gwy=0.0.0.0 prefsrc=10.0.3.59
ci: ref=4 lastused=12 expire=0 err=00000000 used=3 br=0 pmtu=1500

family=02 tab=254 vrf=0 vf=0 type=01 tos=0 flag=00000200
188.172.246.170@3(port1)->10.0.5.7@4(port2) gwy=0.0.0.0 prefsrc=10.0.3.5
ci: ref=1 lastused=24 expire=0 err=00000000 used=0 br=0 pmtu=1500
```

And again, here you can see all the latest routes are saved on the **cache itself**. It doesn't see all the routes that are in the routing table, only the last entries that are frequently used.

FIB

The third-place that your FortiGate checks for routes, if it doesn't actually find anything in the routing cache, or in the policy-based routes is the FIB. The **Forwarding Information Base** holds the active routes, not every route, but only the **Active Routes**. It gets them from the routing table. It also holds routes that are routes that are dedicated to SSL VPN or IPsec. How do you get to see the fib?

"get router info kernel"

```
FortiGate-VM64 # get router info kernel
tab=255 vf=0 scope=253 type=3 proto=2 prio=0 0.0.0.0/0.0.0.0/0->10.0.3.0/
tab=255 vf=0 scope=254 type=2 proto=2 prio=0 0.0.0.0/0.0.0.0/0->10.0.3.59
tab=255 vf=0 scope=253 type=3 proto=2 prio=0 0.0.0.0/0.0.0.0/0->10.0.3.25
tab=255 vf=0 scope=253 type=3 proto=2 prio=0 0.0.0.0/0.0.0.0/0->10.0.5.0/
tab=255 vf=0 scope=254 type=2 proto=2 prio=0 0.0.0.0/0.0.0.0/0->10.0.5.1/
tab=255 vf=0 scope=253 type=3 proto=2 prio=0 0.0.0.0/0.0.0.0/0->10.0.5.25
tab=255 vf=0 scope=253 type=3 proto=2 prio=0 0.0.0.0/0.0.0.0/0->10.0.7.0/
tab=255 vf=0 scope=254 type=2 proto=2 prio=0 0.0.0.0/0.0.0.0/0->10.0.7.1/
tab=255 vf=0 scope=253 type=3 proto=2 prio=0 0.0.0.0/0.0.0.0/0->10.0.7.25
tab=255 vf=0 scope=253 type=3 proto=2 prio=0 0.0.0.0/0.0.0.0/0->127.0.0.0
tab=255 vf=0 scope=254 type=2 proto=2 prio=0 0.0.0.0/0.0.0.0/0->127.0.0.0
tab=255 vf=0 scope=254 type=2 proto=2 prio=0 0.0.0.0/0.0.0.0/0->127.0.0.1
--More--
```

And that's the **FIB**, the third database that your FortiGate checks before it sends the packet towards its destination.

Static **Route**

A static route is Probably the most used route in a FortiGate firewall, It is manually configured and network experts will always tell you, that you can do just about any route using the static route, although you have dynamic routes, (OSPF…) which are much more sophisticated

So in our topology, we have the LAN which is at the **10.0.7.0/24** subnet, we also have our WAN interface which is connected to our router at the **10.0.3.55**

	Name ⇕	Type ⇕	Members ⇕	IP/Netmask ⇕	Administrative Access ⇕
⊟ 📶 **Physical Interface** 🔟					
	📶 LAN (port10)	📶 Physical Interface		10.0.7.1/255.255.255.0	HTTPS SSH
	📶 management (port3)	📶 Physical Interface		10.0.5.1/255.255.255.0	HTTPS SSH HTTP
	📶 port4	📶 Physical Interface		0.0.0.0/0.0.0.0	
	📶 port5	📶 Physical Interface		0.0.0.0/0.0.0.0	
	📶 port6	📶 Physical Interface		0.0.0.0/0.0.0.0	
	📶 port7	📶 Physical Interface		0.0.0.0/0.0.0.0	
	📶 port8	📶 Physical Interface		0.0.0.0/0.0.0.0	
	📶 port9	📶 Physical Interface		0.0.0.0/0.0.0.0	
	📶 ubuntu (port2)	📶 Physical Interface		10.0.4.1/255.255.255.0	PING HTTPS SSH
	📶 WAN (port1)	📶 Physical Interface		10.0.3.55/255.255.255.0	HTTPS HTTP

We need to tell our FortiGate...

" If you see a packet that is coming from the 10.0.7.0 subnet, send it through our WAN interface (the 10.0.3.55) towards our router "

Our static route will be the **default route**

A default Route is the same route that you are getting whenever you connect in your home to your ISP router. which means that any packet that does not have a specific route in your routing table, will be forwarded to the **default route** (your router ISP) as the default Hop

The default route is written in that way 0.0.0.0./0.0.0.0, so let's configure that in our FortiGate

Navigate to **Network — Static Routes**

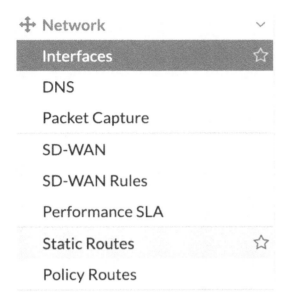

And in static route create a **new static route**, the following screen will appear

Static routes (as dynamic routes) have different attributes that determine if they are **Active or Not**, Preferred more or Less. static route attributes are **Distance and Priority** (available in the advanced options), we will not get to this, in this book, so keep the administrative distance to 10, that is the default setting

- In destination, we will keep the 0.0.0.0/0.0.0.0 which is the default route
- In the interface, we will choose the interface connected to our WAN, which is port 1
- And in gateway address, we will enter, our router GW IP which is connected to our FortiGate, in my case, it is 10.0.3.1

So, we have a **default route** that sends packets to our **WAN** interface, towards our ISP router.

Set Up Policies

Alright, we have our interface all set up, our firewall address object and now we also have a static route, that will let packet flow towards the ISP router on their way to the internet

What is missing? A Policy Of Course

You should think of policy as **"Traffic matching"**, that is, you define a rule that will allow or deny traffic, assuming that it finds a match, once it finds a match (that is your policy), that are a set of things, it can do with that traffic, allow or deny it, save logs, do a network address translation, apply a security policy and more

There are different types of policies in your FortiGate, we will look at the

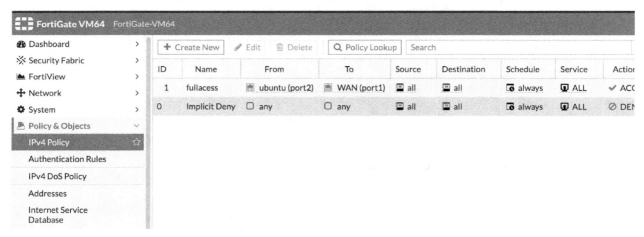

The Most popular ones are IPV4 policies

firewall policies are basically the bread and butter of every firewall.

It doesn't really matter if your firewall is a next-generation firewall. Whenever you head out to the Internet, and you're using a firewall, then you're obliged to firewall rules. What are firewall policies? And how are they made?.

A firewall policy is nothing more than a set of criteria that your traffic needs to match. Whenever an IP session happens in your network, a set of rules are being matched against that traffic. If your firewall doesn't find a match at the first rule, then it goes to the next rule, rules are handled from top to bottom. Now let's look at how our policy rule is being configured and what objects are used to create that match.

In every policy, there's always the implicit deny rule that sits beneath every other rule. That is if your firewall doesn't find any match in the traffic, then the traffic goes to the implicit deny rule, and it is being dropped.

Implicit Deny

So when we start to configure our firewall rule, we have, an implicit deny rule at the bottom. And from there, we start to configure our different criteria that will be matched against your traffic.

We start with the name of the rule itself.

Name
Incoming interface
Outgoing Interface
Source
Destination
schedule
service
action
Implicit Deny

As for naming conventions, don't use too many characters. Don't use spaces between words, try to use underscores.

The second match is the incoming interface. What is the incoming interface? Well, for example, that could be the interface that your local area network is connected to. Wherever the traffic comes from. it could also be your WAN interface

The third match is the outgoing interface.

it can be another segment of your enterprise network, it can be the DMZ or the WAN . the interface that the traffic is heading

The incoming interface is known as the **Ingress interface**.
The outgoing interface is known as the **Egress interface**.

From there we move to the source

Who is the source that generates the traffic? Well, that can be your clients. That can be just about any source that has an IP address, or you can use firewall address objects as **specific IP addresses** within your local area network.
It can also be **a user or user group** that is saved on your firewall, internal database, or a remote authentication server such as LDAP or a RADIUS server.

Another match is the destination

What is the destination that your traffic is heading towards? It can be any destination, an IP address out there, either a specific IP that you can configure or it can be a domain or maybe an internet service as an Amazon service. So be sure to Be granular, don't just use **any or all**. Be specific.

If you're configuring a full access policy that will allow anyone to get out to the internet, then it will probably be "ALL" in the destination field
if you're configuring a specific destination, then be sure to configure them ahead and use them in your policy.

The next match is scheduling

Do you want your policy to work out 24 hours, 7 days? Or do you want it to work on specific hours, specific days, recurring days?
you will probably have cases where you will be asked to open a firewall rule for specific appliances in your local area network. It could be a backup device, it

could be network-attached storage, be sure to know what times those appliances need that firewall rule.

The next match is service

Services are the protocols that are being used in your firewall rule? Are you using only **HTTP, HTTPS, and DNS that is Port 80, Port 443, and Port 53?** Or are you allowing your employees to get out to just about anywhere using any protocol, including **FTP, SSH**, and so on? So again, be careful with the service usage

The last match is action.

Are you denying it? Or are you allowing traffic based on that match?

This was actually the first part of your policy or rule creation.
Once you have a match, your FortiGate will move to your security profiles, which is going through antivirus application control, IPS, and so on.

The other thing that you will have to take care of is are you using network address translation? Are you logging all sessions or only security events?

Alright, so let's configure a policy

Navigate to **Policies and Objects** (you probably guessed it :-), on your left Pane
Create **a new Policy**, and you will see the following screen

Name 🛈	[ ]
Incoming Interface	[▼]
Outgoing Interface	[▼]
Source	[+]
Destination	[+]
Schedule	[🕒 always ▼]
Service	[+]
Action	✔ ACCEPT ⊘ DENY

Inspection Mode   Flow-based Proxy-based

Firewall / Network Options

NAT   🔘

IP Pool Configuration   Use Outgoing Interface Address Use Dynamic IP Pool

Preserve Source Port 🔘

Protocol Options   [PRX default   ▼] ✏

Security Profiles

AntiVirus   🔘

Web Filter   🔘

DNS Filter   🔘

We have said that a policy checks for traffic matching
so let's fill in the missing details

- **Name** your Policy
- The **incoming interface** is our LAN Subnet (which is at port 10)
- The **outgoing interface** is our WAN interface (port 1)
- **Source** — currently choose anyone, but then again, we can also choose, specific devices based on the firewall address objects as My Mac

- **Destination** — again choose all, but you can also limit the destinations to be more specific as well known internet services

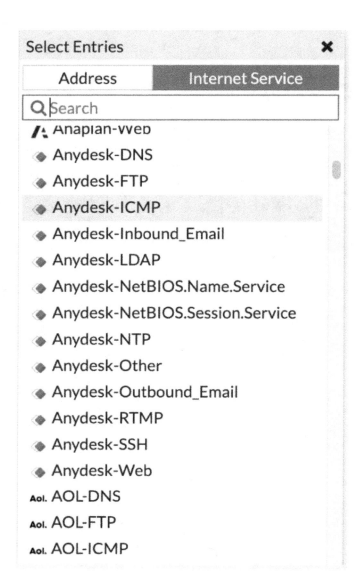

- **Schedule** — you can set your policy to work 24 hours or on different days, in specific hours, as in the case where you need your specific device to backup your hosts
- **Service** — which protocol ? will you allow only HTTPS and DNS or any protocol out there, be granular, so your policies, will not become your back door
- And the last thing is the **ACTION**, which will allow or deny the traffic based on the different matches

Your policy should look something like that

You will see that underneath the matching fields, you can set more settings such as the inspection type (**Flow or Proxy**), NAT, Security Profiles, Logging, and more

Demystify Sessions

Your Fortigate is a session aware firewall, it looks at the first packet that is sent by the source, saves it's routing information, then waits for the responding packet, and only then it creates a session in the session table. Each session has time to live interval, route information, different states, and more

Tracking **Sessions**

The following is a very typical scenario, you have a host, which is part of your local area network. And you want to track its sessions, the places that your host connects to. Now, you can do it in multiple ways you can look at the log report, you can look at the FortiView. But let's do it using the CLI coming up.

So here's the following scenario, you have a device that is part of the 10.0.5.0 subnet. Its IP address is 10.0.5.7 And we want to track its sessions. Now, as I said, we can do it in different ways

So the first command that you can use is the **"get sys session list"**

```
CLI Console                                      ●  🗑  ⭳  📋  ⤢  ✕

FortiGate-VM64 # get system session list
PROTO    EXPIRE  SOURCE              SOURCE-NAT          DESTINATION         DESTINA
igmp     535     10.0.3.1:0          -                   224.0.0.1:0         -
tcp      4       127.0.0.1:20288     -                   127.0.0.1:80        -
tcp      115     10.0.5.7:51344      10.0.3.59:51344     91.189.92.18:443    -
tcp      3599    10.0.5.7:43990      10.0.3.59:43990     91.189.91.38:80     -
tcp      3544    10.0.5.7:38004      10.0.3.59:38004     151.101.194.49:443  -
udp      140     10.0.5.7:60761      10.0.3.59:60761     8.8.8.8:53          -
udp      123     10.0.5.7:51325      10.0.3.59:51325     8.8.8.8:53          -
udp      140     10.0.5.7:56101      10.0.3.59:56101     8.8.8.8:53          -
udp      123     10.0.5.7:48117      10.0.3.59:48117     8.8.8.8:53          -
udp      168     10.0.5.7:48273      10.0.3.59:48273     8.8.8.8:53          -
udp      105     10.0.5.7:45941      10.0.3.59:45941     8.8.8.8:53          -
--More--
```

And from here you can see all the different hosts in your networks and their
different sessions. Now, if you want to be more granular, you can just use the
grep command.

"Get system session list | grep 10.0.5.7"

```
FortiGate-VM64 # get system session list | grep 10.0.5.7
udp      43      10.0.5.7:44269      10.0.3.59:44269     8.8.8.8:53          -
udp      81      10.0.5.7:42505      10.0.3.59:42505     8.8.8.8:53          -
udp      106     10.0.5.7:38189      10.0.3.59:38189     8.8.8.8:53          -
tcp      3553    10.0.5.7:43174      10.0.3.59:43174     37.252.246.101:5938 -
udp      106     10.0.5.7:55194      10.0.3.59:55194     8.8.8.8:53          -
udp      43      10.0.5.7:55991      10.0.3.59:55991     8.8.8.8:53          -
udp      81      10.0.5.7:58340      10.0.3.59:58340     8.8.8.8:53          -

FortiGate-VM64 # ▮
```

And here we can see different sessions that are happening, one of them as you
can see is talking through UDP towards google's DNS server.

Now the other way to do it is using the **"diag sys session list"**

```
FortiGate-VM64 # diag sys session list

session info: proto=2 proto_state=00 duration=25556 expire=427 timeout=
origin-shaper=
reply-shaper=
per_ip_shaper=
class_id=0 ha_id=0 policy_dir=0 tunnel=/ vlan_cos=0/0
state=local may_dirty
statistic(bytes/packets/allow_err): org=68760/1910/1 reply=0/0/0 tuple
tx speed(Bps/kbps): 1/0 rx speed(Bps/kbps): 0/0
orgin->sink: org pre->in, reply out->post dev=11->0/0->11 gwy=0.0.0.0/
hook=pre dir=org act=noop 10.0.3.1:0->224.0.0.1:0(0.0.0.0:0)
hook=post dir=reply act=noop 224.0.0.1:0->10.0.3.1:0(0.0.0.0:0)
misc=0 policy_id=4294967295 auth_info=0 chk_client_info=0 vd=0
serial=00000109 tos=ff/ff app_list=0 app=0 url_cat=0
rpdb_link_id = 00000000 ngfwid=n/a
dd_type=0 dd_mode=0
npu_state=00000000

session info: proto=17 proto_state=01 duration=365 expire=177 timeout=
origin-shaper=
reply-shaper=
per_ip_shaper=
class_id=0 ha_id=0 policy_dir=0 tunnel=/ helper=dns-udp vlan_cos=255/2
state=local nds
statistic(bytes/packets/allow_err): org=1556/24/1 reply=6561/24/1 tuple
tx speed(Bps/kbps): 4/0 rx speed(Bps/kbps): 16/0
orgin->sink: org out->post, reply pre->in dev=0->3/3->13 gwy=0.0.0.0/1
hook=out dir=org act=noop 10.0.3.59:1367->208.91.112.52:53(0.0.0.0:0)
hook=in dir=reply act=noop 208.91.112.52:53->10.0.3.59:1367(0.0.0.0:0)
misc=0 policy_id=0 auth_info=0 chk_client_info=0 vd=0
serial=0000d698 tos=ff/ff app_list=0 app=0 url_cat=0
rpdb_link_id = 00000000 ngfwid=n/a
dd_type=0 dd_mode=0
npu_state=00000000

session info: proto=17 proto_state=01 duration=365 expire=172 timeout=
origin-shaper=
reply-shaper=
per_ip_shaper=
```

As you can see, we have dozens of sessions that are happening just now.

So we will have to use a filter.

Our filter will be the **source address** which is the 10.0.5.7

"Diag sys session filter src 10.0.5.7"

"Diag sys session list "

```
CLI Console                                    ● 🗑 ⬇ 📋 ↗ ✕

FortiGate-VM64 # diag sys session filter src 10.0.5.7

FortiGate-VM64 # diag sys session list █
```

We can filter protocols, destinations, and much more, play around with that,

filtering is a powerful tool

And there we get sessions that are used only by our device

```
CLI Console                                    ● 🗑 ⬇ 📋 ↗ ✕

FortiGate-VM64 # diag sys session filter src 10.0.5.7

FortiGate-VM64 # diag sys session list

session info: proto=6 proto_state=01 duration=700 expire=3569 timeout=360(
origin-shaper=
reply-shaper=
per_ip_shaper=
class_id=0 ha_id=0 policy_dir=0 tunnel=/ vlan_cos=0/255
state=may_dirty
statistic(bytes/packets/allow_err): org=25475/85/1 reply=36706/71/1 tuples
tx speed(Bps/kbps): 3/0 rx speed(Bps/kbps): 2/0
orgin->sink: org pre->post, reply pre->post dev=4->3/3->4 gwy=10.0.3.1/10
hook=post dir=org act=snat 10.0.5.7:43174->37.252.246.101:5938(10.0.3.59:
hook=pre dir=reply act=dnat 37.252.246.101:5938->10.0.3.59:43174(10.0.5.7
pos/(before,after) 0/(0,0), 0/(0,0)
src_mac=00:0c:29:53:1f:c9
misc=0 policy_id=1 auth_info=0 chk_client_info=0 vd=0
serial=0000d51b tos=ff/ff app_list=0 app=0 url_cat=0
rpdb_link_id = 00000000 ngfwid=n/a
dd_type=0 dd_mode=0
npu_state=0x040000
total session 1
```

You can use the grep command again, to filter and be more granular on the different items that you seek such as the type of protocol. Now it's using protocol 6, which is TCP but there are many details on the session output that needs to be clarified

Session **Vocabulary**

When you look at a session output, the first reaction "WOW", what's that, so let's try to analyze the most important ones, and doing so, just look at your session output

You can view your sessions, in different places, one of them is the logs, as long as you enable logs for all sessions on the policy page

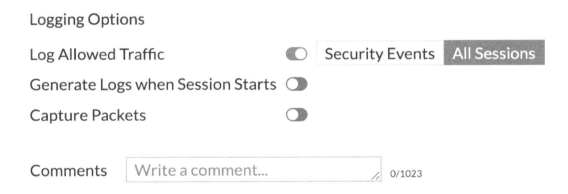

When you move to **Log and report --- Forward Traffic**, you can see all the traffic that moves between your FortiGate interfaces

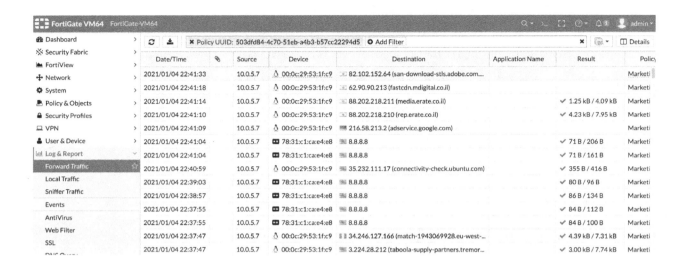

Each line in the logs represents a session

Click on any details and on the top right side, click on **"details"**
You will see the matching session ID

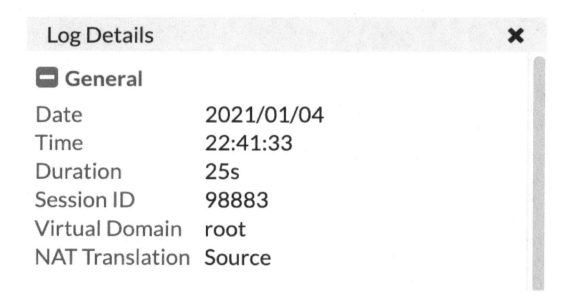

You can get to policy matching logs by **right-clicking** on the policy

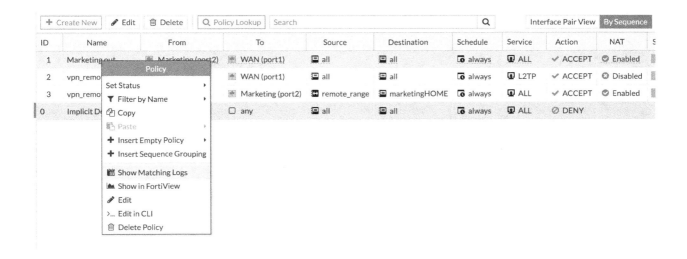

Let's move to our CLI and demystify the session output, we will also filter sessions per policy

Now, we will filter the sessions per policy

"Diag sys session filter policy 1"
"Diag sys session list "

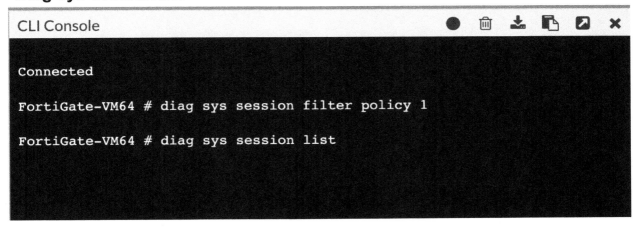

We can see in the button the total number of sessions related to this policy

```
session info: proto=6 proto_state=01 duration=72 expire=3586 timeout=3600 flags=00000000 sockflag=00000000 sockport=0 av_idx=0 use=4
origin-shaper=
reply-shaper=
per_ip_shaper=
class_id=0 ha_id=0 policy_dir=0 tunnel=/ vlan_cos=0/255
state=log may_dirty f00
statistic(bytes/packets/allow_err): org=3629/19/1 reply=5774/16/1 tuples=2
tx speed(Bps/kbps): 49/0 rx speed(Bps/kbps): 79/0
origin->sink: org pre->post, reply pre->post dev=4->3/3->4 gwy=10.0.3.1/10.0.5.7
hook=post dir=org act=snat 10.0.5.7:54484->216.58.204.14:443(10.0.3.59:54484)
hook=pre dir=reply act=dnat 216.58.204.14:443->10.0.3.59:54484(10.0.5.7:54484)
pos/(before,after) 0/(0,0), 0/(0,0)
src_mac=00:0c:29:53:1f:c9
misc=0 policy_id=1 auth_info=0 chk_client_info=0 vd=0
serial=0001791d tos=ff/ff app_list=0 app=0 url_cat=0
rpdb_link_id = 00000000 ngfwid=n/a
dd_type=0 dd_mode=0
npu_state=0x040000
total session 26
```

In the session state, we see that it is equal to log, which means, that the session is being logged

Session proto

It is the protocol used, it has a numbering index where:

- **6=TCP**
- **17=UDP**
- **1=ICMP**

You can find the full list using google, but these are probably the main ones that you will meet

Session State

Following the protocol that is used, comes the protocol state. Again there is a numbering index, but before that, think of a regular 3 way TCP handshake
A client sends a SYN packet, The server responds with a SYN/ACK the client returns an ACK. When it wants to finish the connection, it sends a FIN packet, and so on

State	Value	Expire Timer (default)
NONE	0	10 s
ESTABLISHED	1	3600 s
SYN_SENT	2	120 s
SYN & SYN/ACK	3	60 s
FIN_WAIT	4	120 s
TIME_WAIT	5	1 s
CLOSE	6	10 s
CLOSE_WAIT	7	120 s
LAST_ACK	8	30 s
LISTEN	9	120 s

Following the state, you will find the expiration time, the duration of that session, these are self-explanatory

If you are using a traffic shaping policy, then you will notice that on the origin shaper fields

```
origin-shaper=
reply-shaper=
per_ip_shaper=
```

May **Dirty**

The next interesting part is the state where it shows up = may dirty. there could be 2 states, either **dirty** or **may dirty**

```
state=log may_dirty
```

When it is dirty, the session needs to be validated again.

When your FortiGate receives the first packet, it evaluates the packet according to the policy. the evaluation is usually done on the first packet only

But if throughout the session, the firewall policy changes, routing changes, or network configuration is done, it is re-evaluated again

If the packet follows the policies, then it is labeled **"may dirty"**

When a policy changes or any other condition, then the state for the following packets changes to **"dirty "**

Your FortiGate checks the packets again, and only then- it changes the state to may dirty again

Session **TTL**

When a user doesn't perform any action throughout a session, this session will time out.

Each session and its protocol has a different interval on your FortiGate firewall. A TCP session by default will timeout after 3600 seconds. But there are cases such as in the medical world where you need your services, your sessions, not to time out. How do you do it using a policy? And how do you do with using a custom service?

Before we configure the session timeout, we will configure it on port 443. Let's take a look at our Ubuntu device. Let's just resume it and let's refresh the page. We're at YouTube. Alright, let's go back and let's just use the "diag sys session list"

We can take a look at sessions that are TCP sessions, we can see that we have an expiration time of 3600 seconds. Now let's configure a custom service Using the **"config firewall service custom"**

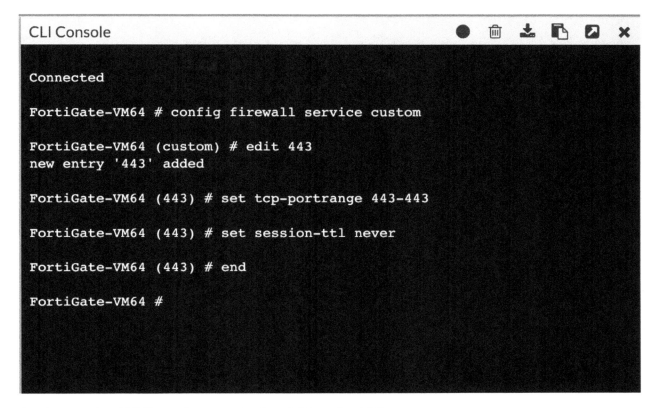

```
CLI Console                                    ●  🗑  ⬇  📋  ↗  ✕

Connected

FortiGate-VM64 # config firewall service custom

FortiGate-VM64 (custom) # edit 443
new entry '443' added

FortiGate-VM64 (443) # set tcp-portrange 443-443

FortiGate-VM64 (443) # set session-ttl never

FortiGate-VM64 (443) # end

FortiGate-VM64 #
```

Let's set the TCP port range to be 443 only 443.

And let's set the session Time To Live to never.

Now let's end it

And you can also see the new service under the Services tab and categorized services that we have just created.

| 🖵 443 | TCP/443 | 0.0.0.0 | ✓ Visible |

Log And Report

Logs are fundamental to your FortiGate Administration. Let's look at the log structure and understand how that works.

You can look at the different logs using the graphical user interface in the log and report menu.

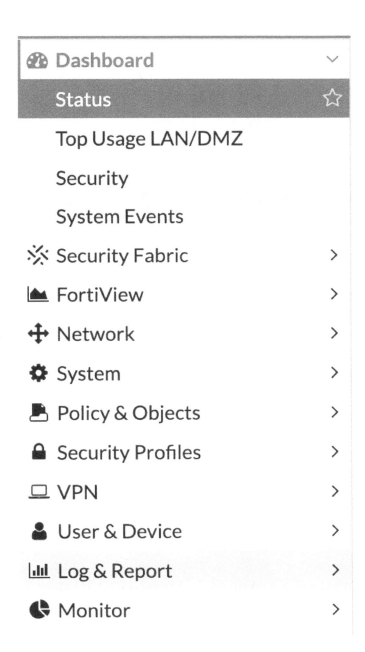

From there, you will see the different logs as forward traffic logs which track, traffic that flows between your FortiGate interfaces

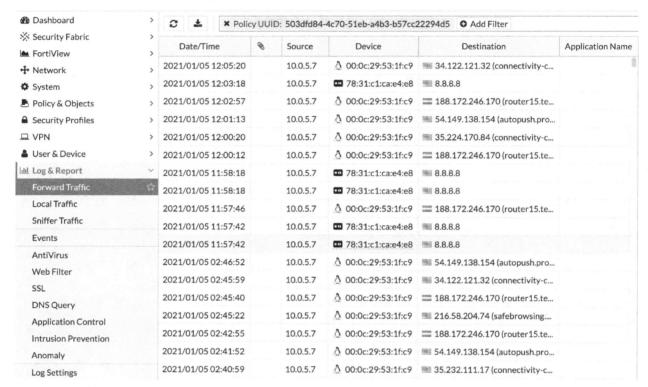

Local traffic, which is internal traffic, sniffer traffic, if you're using packet capture, and from there, you can see the different security profile logs.

To see logs either security logs or every session log, you have to enable logs in your policy.

Enable Logs **on policy**

let's move to my policy and scroll down where I can enable log allowed traffic to either all sessions or security events.

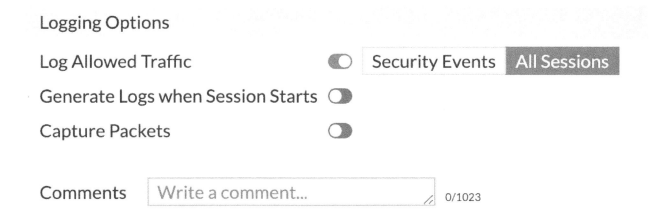

I've enabled it on all sessions. So let's just move to my Ubuntu device. Let's create let's generate some traffic, let's open up YouTube

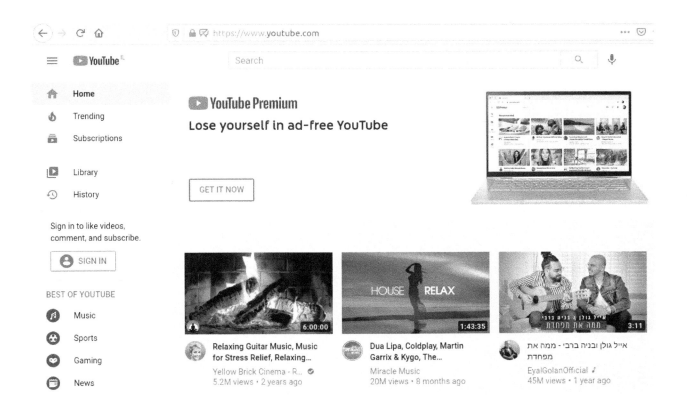

let's move back to my **Log and Report** page.

Understand Logs **Through Commands**

Our traffic actually flows through the policy that we have created. So we can look at the forward traffic we have all the details, we can look at the source IP at the destination itself, we can also look at the application name.

 And if we click one of the logs, we can see that we have much more details, either in terms of the action that the policy took or the application that was used, we can also see the security level that was used.

Now, you do not have to use just about any **security level** out there. So let's move to our command line

"config Log disk filter"

```
FortiGate-VM64 # config log disk filter

FortiGate-VM64 (filter) # show full-configuration
config log disk filter
    set severity information
    set forward-traffic enable
    set local-traffic enable
    set multicast-traffic enable
    set sniffer-traffic enable
    set anomaly enable
    set voip enable
    set dlp-archive enable
    set gtp enable
    set filter ''
    set filter-type include
end

FortiGate-VM64 (filter) #
```

if you use the **"show full config"** , you will see that you have different severity
levels :

1. Emergency
2. Alert
3. Critical
4. Error
5. Warning
6. Notification
7. Information
8. debug

Let's set the severity to **critical** so that logs that will be saved are only those in
critical severity level and anything that is above it.

```
FortiGate-VM64 # config log disk filter

FortiGate-VM64 (filter) # show full-configuration
config log disk filter
    set severity information
    set forward-traffic enable
    set local-traffic enable
    set multicast-traffic enable
    set sniffer-traffic enable
    set anomaly enable
    set voip enable
    set dlp-archive enable
    set gtp enable
    set filter ''
    set filter-type include
end

FortiGate-VM64 (filter) # set severity critical█
```

Download Your **Logs**

Getting back to our GUI logs. if we will click on the **download** logs (the second button from the left)

Date/Time	📎	Source	Device	Destination
			Policy UUID: 503dfd84-4c70-51eb-a4b3-b57cc22294d5 ⊕ Add Filter	
2021/01/05 12:22:15		10.0.5.7	🐧 00:0c:29:53:1f:c9	188.172.246.170 (router15.te...
2021/01/05 12:22:04		10.0.5.7	🐧 00:0c:29:53:1f:c9	216.58.206.110 (youtube-ui.l....
2021/01/05 12:21:14		10.0.5.7	🐧 00:0c:29:53:1f:c9	54.149.138.154 (autopush.pro...

We can actually open the different logs once downloaded, let's just pick up one log event

```
date=2021-01-05 time=12:23:18 logid="0000000013"
srcintfrole="lan" dstip=8.8.8.8 dstport=53 dstin
service="DNS" dstcountry="United States" srccoun
duration=180 sentbyte=86 rcvdbyte=134 sentpkt=1
```

Let's look at the structure of the log. The log is actually comprised of two parts:

header **part**

The header part is similar in all logs, the body part is different

```
date=2021-01-05 time=12:23:18 logid="0000000013" type="traffic" subtype="forward" level="notice" vd="root"
```

In the header, we can see the date, the log ID, the type of traffic, the subtype, which is forward traffic, the severity level, which is only "notice", and the Vdom that we are working on which currently is the root Vdom

The body **part**

In the body, we will see the event time we will see the source IP that triggers the traffic, the source port the interface that it is connected, the destination IP, the policy that we have used, and the type of protocol number (17 is UDP)

```
eventtime=1609878198525583743 tz="-0800" srcip=10.0.5.7 srcport=51275 srcintf="port2"
on="accept" policyid=1 policytype="policy" poluuid="503dfd84-4c70-51eb-a4b3-b57cc22294d5"
```

We will also see the action that was done. For example, if you see **"client rst"**, it means that the server sent a TCP reset message to the client.

```
proto=17 action="accept" policyid=1 polic
.59 transport=51275 appid=16195 app="DNS"
```

Log **settings**

Another good command that you will probably use is the

"config log disk setting"

```
FortiGate-VM64 # config log disk setting

FortiGate-VM64 (setting) # show full-configuration
config log disk setting
    set status enable
    set ips-archive enable
    set max-policy-packet-capture-size 100
    set log-quota 0
    set dlp-archive-quota 0
    set report-quota 0
    set maximum-log-age 7
    set upload disable
    set full-first-warning-threshold 75
    set full-second-warning-threshold 90
    set full-final-warning-threshold 95
    set max-log-file-size 20
    set roll-schedule daily
    set roll-time 00:00
    set diskfull overwrite
end

FortiGate-VM64 (setting) # 
```

Now here you can set different settings that are related to your logs. One of them
is the maximum log age, which currently by default is seven days and you can
change it. It all depends on your hard disk and its storage.
Play around with the different settings, understand your logs capabilities, it's
crucial to your everyday administration

Delete **Logs**

The last command is the

"execute log delete-all "

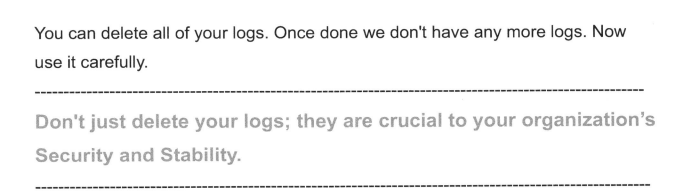

```
FortiGate-VM64 # exe FortiGate-VM64 #
FortiGate-VM64 # execute log delete-all
```

You can delete all of your logs. Once done we don't have any more logs. Now use it carefully.

Don't just delete your logs; they are crucial to your organization's Security and Stability.

Memory Optimization

Your firewall memory is a precious resource that you need to understand and master. how your memory is distributed, how it managed, and what can you learn from simple diagnostic commands

Memory in your Firewall is being allocated between the kernel, system i / o cache, the different buffers, and the shared memory. we will also cover how you can optimize your memory utilization for maximum performance.

Memory utilization and Memory optimization are one of the key fundamentals that every network administrator should master.

Your firewall Memory actually is being distributed between the kernel, the buffers, the processes, between many operations that are on your firewall hardware and software architecture.

Let's take a look at one memory component which is the **slab** or the **slabs** - these are memory objects that are used by your kernel.

Type **"diag hardware sysinfo slab"**

```
CLI Console                                    ⏺  🗑  ⬇  📋  ⬈

Connected

FortiGate-VM64 # diag hardware sysinfo slab
slabinfo - version: 2.1
# name              <active_objs> <num_objs> <objsize> <objperslab> <pag
tcp6_session              6         6      1344     3      1 : tunables   60    30
ip6_session               0         0      1280     3      1 : tunables   60    30
sctp_session              0         0      1536     5      2 : tunables   60    30
tcp_session               6        15      1408     5      2 : tunables   60    30
ip_session             1164      1170      1344     3      1 : tunables   60    30
fib6_nodes               10        59        64    59      1 : tunables  252   126
ip6_dst_cache            34        60       384    10      1 : tunables  124    62
ndisc_cache               3        24       320    12      1 : tunables  124    62
ip6_mrt_cache             0         0       128    30      1 : tunables  252   126
RAWv6                   133       136      1024     4      1 : tunables  124    62
UDPLITEv6                 0         0      1024     4      1 : tunables  124    62
UDPv6                    10        12      1024     4      1 : tunables  124    62
tw_sock_TCPv6             8        12       320    12      1 : tunables  124    62
request_sock_TCPv6        8        20       192    20      1 : tunables  252   126
TCPv6                    26        26      1792     2      1 : tunables   60    30
uhci_urb_priv             0         0        56    67      1 : tunables  252   126
scsi_sense_cache         30        30       128    30      1 : tunables  252   126
scsi_cmd_cache           30        30       256    15      1 : tunables  252   126
sd_ext_cdb                2       112        32   112      1 : tunables  252   126
cfq_io_context           50        60       128    30      1 : tunables  252   126
cfq_queue                50        68       232    17      1 : tunables  252   126
hugetlbfs_inode_cache     1         7       528     7      1 : tunables  124
isofs_inode_cache         0         0       560     7      1 : tunables  124    62
fat_inode_cache           0         0       616     6      1 : tunables  124    62
fat_cache                 0         0        32   112      1 : tunables  252   126
journal_handle            0         0        24   144      1 : tunables  252   126
journal_head              0         0       112    34      1 : tunables  252   126
revoke_table              2       202        16   202      1 : tunables  252   126
revoke_record             0         0        32   112      1 : tunables  252   126
ext2_inode_cache        334       340       696     5      1 : tunables  124    62
```

On the following output, you will see all the memory objects that your kernel holds. Those could be TCP sessions, IP sessions, Routes that are used in the cache.

On the left side, you can see the slab name, the size of the slab, and the number of slab objects.

# name	<active_objs>	<num_objs>	<objsize
tcp6_session	6	6	1344	3	1 :
ip6_session	0	0	1280	3	1 :
sctp_session	0	0	1536	5	2 :
tcp_session	6	15	1408	5	2 :
ip_session	1164	1170	1344	3	1 :
fib6_nodes	10	59	64	59	1 :
ip6_dst_cache	34	60	384	10	1 :
ndisc_cache	3	24	320	12	1 :
ip6_mrt_cache	0	0	128	30	1 :
RAWv6	133	136	1024	4	1 :
UDPLITEv6	0	0	1024	4	1 :
UDPv6	10	12	1024	4	1 :
tw_sock_TCPv6	8	12	320	12	1 :

And this is only one place where your firewall reserves memory.

The second command is the **"diag hardware sysinfo "**

```
FortiGate-VM64 # diag hardware sysinfo memory
MemTotal:          1012200 kB
MemFree:             94580 kB
Buffers:                72 kB
Cached:             466492 kB
SwapCached:              0 kB
Active:             283484 kB
Inactive:           290292 kB
Active(anon):       283444 kB
Inactive(anon):     289660 kB
Active(file):           40 kB
Inactive(file):        632 kB
Unevictable:        149180 kB
Mlocked:                 0 kB
SwapTotal:               0 kB
SwapFree:                0 kB
Dirty:                   0 kB
Writeback:               0 kB
AnonPages:          256428 kB
Mapped:              96568 kB
Shmem:              316676 kB
Slab:                54456 kB
SReclaimable:         7920 kB
SUnreclaim:          46536 kB
```

Here we have two subsets of the command:

A.The memory — **"diag hardware sysinfo memory**
B. the shared memory — **"diag hardware sysinfo sh"**

Using the first option, you will see the:

- The total amount of memory:

- The free memory

- The memory that is used by the buffer

- The memory that is used by the cached system i/o operation.

The last piece of information is very important.

```
Cached:            466492  kB
SwapCached:             0  kB
Active:            283484  kB
Inactive:          290292  kB
```

Your system input and output use Memory cache very often for logging events, explicit proxy, WAN optimization. **cache** is used everywhere on your FortiGate.

The **active cache memory** is for operations that are used often, the inactive, is for those that are not.

Let's move to shared memory command **"diag hardware sysinfo sh "**

```
FortiGate-VM64 # diag hardware sysinfo sh
SHM FS total:          556589056          530 MB
SHM FS free:           556249088          530 MB
SHM FS avail:          556249088          530 MB
SHM FS alloc:             339968            0 MB

FortiGate-VM64 # ▉
```

The output shows memory that is being shared by processes.

Processes have their own memory allocation, a process cannot just get into another process memory allocation. It lives on its own proprietary memory allocation. But there are different operations that your FortiGate actually allocates a specific shared memory for different processes to reach. And those can be seen using the **"diag hardware sysinfo sh "**

Another command is the "diag sys top"

```
FortiGate-VM64 # diag sys top
Run Time:  1 days, 15 hours and 12 minutes
0U, 0N, 0S, 100I, 0WA, 0HI, 0SI, 0ST; 988T, 90F
            httpsd    10209      S        0.5     3.9
            cmdbsvr      134     S        0.0     4.2
            reportd      175     S        0.0     3.9
           forticron     167     S        0.0     3.5
            httpsd    10194      S        0.0     3.3
            httpsd    10151      S        0.0     3.3
            httpsd    10199      S        0.0     3.2
            httpsd    10198      S        0.0     2.8
            httpsd    10219      S        0.0     2.8
            src-vis      687     S        0.0     2.8
           ipshelper     191     S <      0.0     2.6
            cw_acd       187     S        0.0     2.5
            newcli    10245      S        0.0     2.5
            httpsd       159     S        0.0     2.5
           ipsengine    6433     S <      0.0     2.4
           dnsproxy      184     S        0.0     1.8
            miglogd      203     S        0.0     1.8
            miglogd      157     S        0.0     1.8
            fgfmd       9358     S        0.0     1.8
    initXXXXXXXXXXX        1     S        0.0     1.7
```

The **sys top** command (similar to the top command on Linux)
is often used to show the different processes that are used on
your FortiGate firewall and the memory allocation for each
process.

You will most likely see processes that consume lots of memory,
such as the IPS, you will also see processes as the HTTPSD,
the HTTPS daemon, which is actually the graphical user

interface that we work on, the repeating HTTPSD processes are actually child processes. So there is not only one process, there's the parent process, and there are child processes.

Memory optimization **tips**

Memory optimization can be done in many ways, we will look at a few.

- Don't just log anything on your firewall policies. There are cases when you need to log security events. There are cases when you need to log all sessions. Do that according to your needs.

Logging Options		
Log Allowed Traffic	🔘 **Security Events**	All Sessions
Generate Logs when Session Starts	🔘	
Capture Packets	🔘	

- Don't apply any security profiles out there, just because you can

Your IPS (intrusion prevention system) as an example is one of the most resource-consuming features. it parses and decodes

Different protocols used in your network traffic, it looks for patterns and for anomalies. So use it carefully, If you're having a network that consists of only Windows machines or Windows servers don't use signatures that are targeted at Linux OS or Mac OS, **use your IPS very carefully.**

- The next thing that you will need to know is about session Time To Live. Your session table by default holds sessions for up to an hour. That is not necessary in most cases. And here, you can actually use the **"config system session-ttl "** to change the default setting

```
FortiGate-VM64 # config system session-ttl

FortiGate-VM64 (session-ttl) # set default 800
```

The default currently is 3600 seconds, you can set it to 600 seconds, in most cases, that will be enough

- You can also configure that on a firewall specific policy or even on a specific service. here you will use the **"config firewall service custom"**

let's just name this service **"custom"** and configure the TCP port range of the service and the session time to live

```
FortiGate-VM64 # config firewall service custom

FortiGate-VM64 (custom) # edit "custom"
new entry 'custom' added

FortiGate-VM64 (custom) # set tcp-portrange 433

FortiGate-VM64 (custom) # set session-ttl
```

Useful CLI Commands

fortigate commands are built as a tree

with 5 main branches

- config
- show
- get
- diag
- Execute

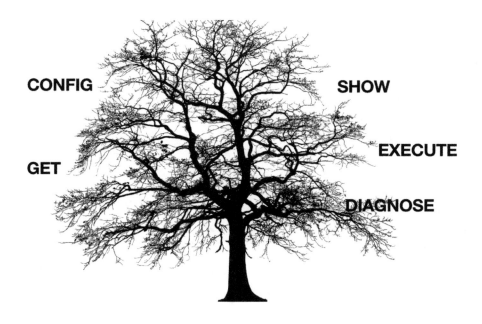

Each branch has its purpose, for example

config allows you to configure objects

one object is system

In the system object, you have sub-objects such as:

- administrators
- DNS
- interfaces
- routes

To configure those sub-objects, you will use subcommands such as :

- set (assign values)
- edit (add or edit a specific entry)

The configuration table is built from variables and values and if you want to have a look at the table contents (members), you will use the **get command**

Another command, the **show** command will list the changes to the default configuration

The following commands are helpful to monitor and diagnose your fortigate firewall

"Get system status"

Shows your fortigate set up, including firmware version, security profile database dates, license validity, Vdom used, HA participation, and more

```
FortiGate-VM64 # get system status
Version: FortiGate-VM64 v6.2.5,build1142,200819 (GA)
Virus-DB: 1.00000(2018-04-09 18:07)
Extended DB: 1.00000(2018-04-09 18:07)
Extreme DB: 1.00000(2018-04-09 18:07)
IPS-DB: 6.00741(2015-12-01 02:30)
IPS-ETDB: 0.00000(2001-01-01 00:00)
APP-DB: 6.00741(2015-12-01 02:30)
INDUSTRIAL-DB: 6.00741(2015-12-01 02:30)
Serial-Number: FGVMEVGJZRZOVX3F
IPS Malicious URL Database: 1.00001(2015-01-01 01:01)
Botnet DB: 1.00000(2012-05-28 22:51)
License Status: Valid
Evaluation License Expires: Thu Jan 14 04:10:33 2021
VM Resources: 1 CPU/1 allowed, 1998 MB RAM/2048 MB allowed
Log hard disk: Available
Hostname: FortiGate-VM64
Operation Mode: NAT
Current virtual domain: root
Max number of virtual domains: 1
Virtual domains status: 1 in NAT mode, 0 in TP mode
Virtual domain configuration: disable
FIPS-CC mode: disable
Current HA mode: standalone
Branch point: 1142
--More--
```

"Diag sys top"

Shows the different processes that are running on your Fortigate. Useful to monitor resource-intensive processes as the IPS

```
FortiGate-VM64 # diag sys top
Run Time:   1 days, 9 hours and 4 minutes
0U, 0N, 0S, 100I, 0WA, 0HI, 0SI, 0ST; 1998T, 993F
        reportd      175      S        0.0      2.4
      ipshelper      197      S <      0.0      1.8
         httpsd     9000      S        0.0      1.7
       forticron     167      S        0.0      1.7
      ipsengine     5526      S <      0.0      1.6
         httpsd     9067      S        0.0      1.6
         httpsd     9075      S        0.0      1.6
         httpsd     9089      S        0.0      1.5
            wad     8575      S        0.0      1.5
        src-vis      185      S        0.0      1.4
         httpsd     9059      S        0.0      1.3
         httpsd     9090      S        0.0      1.3
         cmdbsvr     136      S        0.0      1.3
         cw_acd      193      S        0.0      1.2
         newcli     9057      S        0.0      1.2
         httpsd      159      S        0.0      1.2
        miglogd      213      S        0.0      0.9
        miglogd      157      S        0.0      0.9
            wad     8574      S        0.0      0.9
          fgfmd     8738      S        0.0      0.9
```

"diag sniffer packet <interface> <'filter'> <verbose> <count> a"

This command will capture packets on your fortigate , you can set up the
interface, protocol, source, destination, verbosity level and more

```
FortiGate-VM64 # diag sniffer packet any
interfaces=[any]
filters=[none]
1.072492 10.0.3.59.80 -> 10.0.3.22.59317: psh 3687427693 ack 1593291339
1.072738 10.0.3.22.59317 -> 10.0.3.59.80: ack 3687428071
1.075062 10.0.3.22.59317 -> 10.0.3.59.80: psh 1593291339 ack 3687428071
1.075083 10.0.3.59.80 -> 10.0.3.22.59317: ack 1593292503
1.611723 10.0.5.7.46422 -> 217.146.14.133.5938: psh 1469699392 ack 2073
1.611883 10.0.3.59.46422 -> 217.146.14.133.5938: psh 1469699392 ack 207
1.730285 217.146.14.133.5938 -> 10.0.3.59.46422: psh 2073376514 ack 146
1.730399 217.146.14.133.5938 -> 10.0.5.7.46422: psh 2073376514 ack 1469
1.730920 10.0.5.7.46422 -> 217.146.14.133.5938: ack 2073376538
1.730968 10.0.3.59.46422 -> 217.146.14.133.5938: ack 2073376538
2.072644 10.0.3.59.80 -> 10.0.3.22.59317: psh 3687428071 ack 1593292503
2.072865 10.0.3.22.59317 -> 10.0.3.59.80: ack 3687429153
```

"get sys seesion list"

We have used this command, it will show up the different sessions that are
running on your fortigate, including the NAT (network address translation used)

```
FortiGate-VM64 # get system session list
PROTO   EXPIRE SOURCE              SOURCE-NAT          DESTINATION          DES
igmp    551    10.0.3.1:0          -                   224.0.0.1:0          -
tcp     3590   10.0.5.7:32926      10.0.3.59:32926     52.41.198.156:443 -
udp     170    10.0.5.7:50325      10.0.3.59:50325     8.8.8.8:53           -
udp     170    10.0.5.7:41865      10.0.3.59:41865     8.8.8.8:53           -
udp     120    10.0.5.7:42213      10.0.3.59:42213     8.8.8.8:53           -
udp     170    10.0.5.7:48485      10.0.3.59:48485     8.8.8.8:53           -
udp     175    10.0.5.7:50017      10.0.3.59:50017     91.189.91.157:123 -
udp     170    10.0.5.7:51394      10.0.3.59:51394     8.8.8.8:53           -
tcp     3568   10.0.5.7:46422      10.0.3.59:46422     217.146.14.133:5938
udp     174    10.0.3.59:1048      -                   208.91.112.52:53 -
udp     179    10.0.3.59:1048      -                   208.91.112.53:53 -
--More--
```

"Diag ip address list"

Shows up the IP addresses that are used on different interfaces

```
FortiGate-VM64 # diag ip address list
IP=10.0.3.59->10.0.3.59/255.255.255.0 index=3 devname=port1
IP=10.0.5.1->10.0.5.1/255.255.255.0 index=4 devname=port2
IP=10.0.7.1->10.0.7.1/255.255.255.0 index=5 devname=port3
IP=127.0.0.1->127.0.0.1/255.0.0.0 index=13 devname=root
IP=127.0.0.1->127.0.0.1/255.0.0.0 index=16 devname=vsys_ha
IP=127.0.0.1->127.0.0.1/255.0.0.0 index=18 devname=vsys_fgfm
IP=10.0.2.1->10.0.2.1/255.255.255.0 index=19 devname=vlan100
```

"Diag user device list"

Shows up the users and devices used on your network

```
FortiGate-VM64 # diag user device list
hosts
  vd root/0   78:31:c1:ca:e4:e8   gen 1152   req OHUSA/3e
    created 119539s   gen 2   seen 7s   port2   gen 2
    ip 10.0.3.22   src arp
    hardware vendor 'Apple'   src mac   id 0   weight 120
  vd root/0   80:86:d9:ad:0f:04   gen 45   req OHUSA/3e
    created 102771s   gen 45   seen 60735s   port2   gen 17
  vd root/0   c0:84:7d:65:f5:77   gen 16   req OHUSA/3e
    created 119427s   gen 15   seen 714s   port2   gen 8
    ip 10.0.3.89   src mac
  vd root/0   3c:bd:3e:c4:2f:3a   gen 30   req OHUA/3c
    created 119469s   gen 13   seen 161s   port2   gen 7
    ip 10.0.3.171   src mac
    os 'Android'   src dhcp   id 845   weight 128
    software version '8.0.0'   src dhcp   id 845   weight 128
  vd root/0   00:0c:29:df:6d:aa   gen 998   req OHUSA/3e
    created 119539s   gen 3   seen 6512s   port2   gen 3
    ip 10.0.3.59   src arp
```

"execute ping-options"

Troubleshoot connectivity using ICMP packets. This command has different
options as count, interval, source, and more

```
FortiGate-VM64 # execute ping google.com
PING google.com (172.217.22.46): 56 data bytes
64 bytes from 172.217.22.46: icmp_seq=0 ttl=110 time=83.7 ms
64 bytes from 172.217.22.46: icmp_seq=1 ttl=110 time=83.2 ms
64 bytes from 172.217.22.46: icmp_seq=2 ttl=110 time=83.8 ms
64 bytes from 172.217.22.46: icmp_seq=3 ttl=110 time=83.8 ms
64 bytes from 172.217.22.46: icmp_seq=4 ttl=110 time=83.8 ms

--- google.com ping statistics ---
5 packets transmitted, 5 packets received, 0% packet loss
round-trip min/avg/max = 83.2/83.6/83.8 ms

FortiGate-VM64 #
```

"Show system interface port(x)"

Shows the current configuration on different interfaces

```
FortiGate-VM64 # show system interface port1
config system interface
    edit "port1"
        set vdom "root"
        set ip 10.0.3.59 255.255.255.0
        set allowaccess https http
        set type physical
        set alias "WAN"
        set lldp-reception enable
        set role wan
        set snmp-index 1
    next
end
```

"Get system arp"

Shows the ARP table on your FortiGate

```
FortiGate-VM64 # get system arp
Address              Age(min)     Hardware Addr       Interface
10.0.3.22            0            78:31:c1:ca:e4:e8   port1
10.0.5.7             0            00:0c:29:53:1f:c9   port2
10.0.3.1             0            a4:91:b1:78:d7:d9   port1

FortiGate-VM64 #
```

"Diag hardware deviceinfo nic port(X)"

Shows the MAC address and the state of interfaces (speed, MTU size…)

```
FortiGate-VM64 # diag hardware deviceinfo nic port1
Name:             port1
Driver:           e1000
Version:          7.3.21-k8-NAPI
Bus:              0000:02:00.0
Hwaddr:           00:0c:29:df:6d:aa
Permanent Hwaddr:00:0c:29:df:6d:aa
State:            up
Link:             up
Mtu:              1500
Supported:        auto 10half 10full 100half 100full 1000full
Advertised:       auto 10half 10full 100half 100full 1000full
Speed:            1000full
Auto:             enabled
RX Ring:                 256
TX Ring:                 256
Rx packets:              453313
Rx bytes:                320849978
Rx compressed:           0
```

Virtual Domains

How do you take your single FortiGate split into several virtual domains, several virtual appliances, each with their own firewall policies each with their own administrators?

Why do you need VDOM's? the short answer is that you can divide different customers or different sections in your organization, into different domains as if each has its own FortiGate firewall.

Your FortiGate support virtual domains, in several modes, the most used is Multi VDOM Mode, so let's look at the steps involved

In the following Example Our Fortigate currently has 2 interfaces configured

⊟ ▦ Physical Interface 10			
▦ LAN (port2)	▦ Physical Interface	10.0.5.1/255.255.255.0	PING HTTPS
▦ port1	▦ Physical Interface	192.168.1.55/255.255.255.0	HTTPS HTTP
▦ port3	▦ Physical Interface	0.0.0.0/0.0.0.0	
▦ port4	▦ Physical Interface	0.0.0.0/0.0.0.0	
▦ port5	▦ Physical Interface	0.0.0.0/0.0.0.0	

We will create a new VDOM and assign the LAN interface (10.0.5.0) to it

Configure new VDOM's can be done in several models from the GUI, but we will do it using the command line.

And the command is:

```
CLI Console (1) ✎

FGVM00TM21001252 # config system global

FGVM00TM21001252 (global) # set vdom-mode multi-vdom

FGVM00TM21001252 (global) # end
You will be logged out for the operation to take effect.
Do you want to continue? (y/n)y

█
```

Your Fortigate will not reboot. It will only log you out.

Once you enter again. you will see graphical interface changes

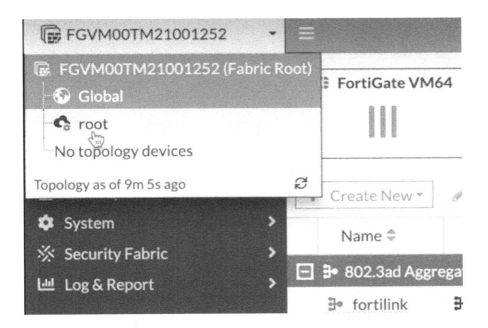

On the left side, you can move between the different VDOM's which we have not yet configured.

We currently have only the basic root VDOM.

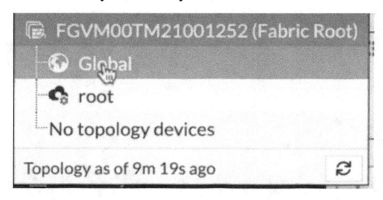

let's create our first VDOM. And allocate resources, interfaces and create links between them.

To do so, you will need to move to the global VDOM ------- system. And press on the VDOM menu

As shown, our root VDOM is the Management VDOM it works on a profile-based NGFW Mode, currently all interfaces are associated with the Root VDOM, its operation mode is NAT and you can also see the utilization of resources and the interfaces (CPU and Memory)

CPU ⇕	Memory ⇕
0%	51%

So let's create a new virtual domain. Click the **"Create New"** Button, Let's name our virtual domain "Marketing", as it will deal with the marketing division. NGFW mode will be profile-based, we will keep the Wi-Fi country region the same for the United States.

And we have created our new virtual domain which is for the marketing division.

The second thing that we will need to do is to allocate interfaces for that virtual domain. If we'll move to network interfaces, you will see that there are no interfaces allocated to that virtual domain.

So let's just do that.

Let's move back to global network interfaces (on the top left side, press and move to **"Global"**)

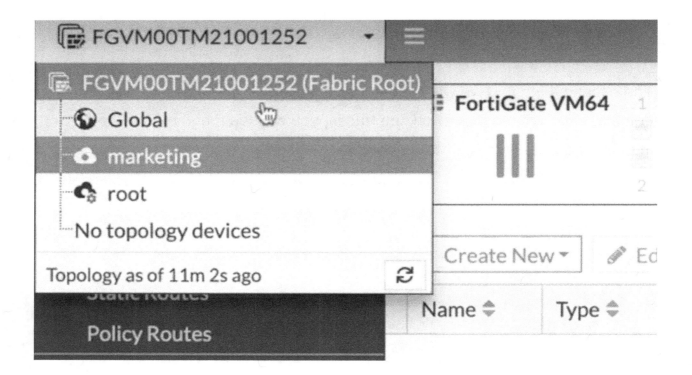

And let's allocate the LAN interface to our new VDOM.

Move to Interfaces

Press on any interface, that you wish to allocate to the new Marketing VDOM. in our case this will be port 2 --- **edit**

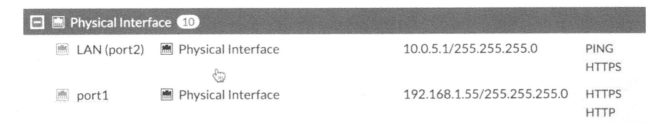

And here we have a new field which is the virtual domain field.

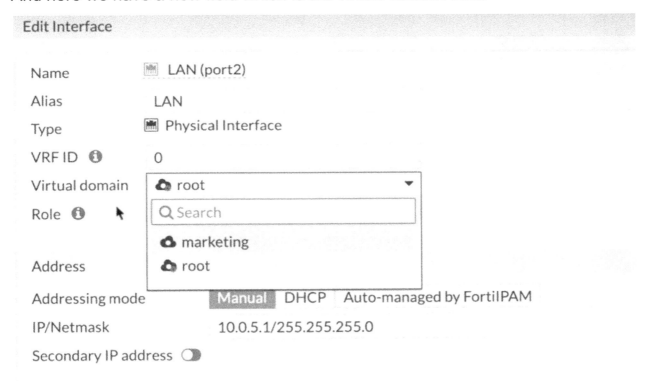

We will assign port 2 to our marketing division VDOM . and let's move back to our marketing VDOM and look at the interfaces and we have a new interface that is allocated to that specific VDOM,

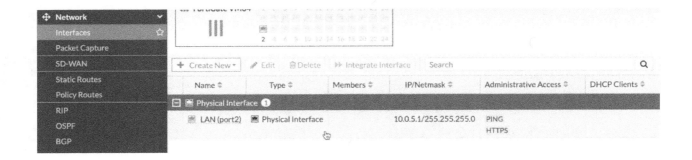

Now that we have our new VDOM, we need to create or configure a new administrator that will take care of it.

We will need to move back to global VDOM (which takes care as you already understand, for all the management stuff) ---- system administrator

Click New admin. name him marketing admin, choose a password. For the administrator, profile choose professional admin, as he is only responsible for that specific VDOM, and assign him to our new marketing VDOM

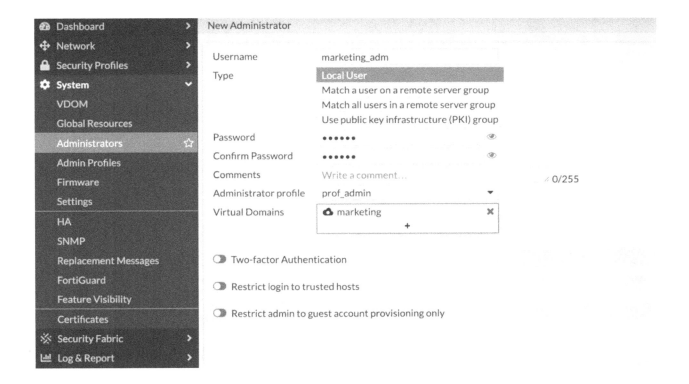

Now we have two administrators, we have the super admin which takes care of all the VDOM's. With full writing and reading permissions And we have a new professional admin that takes care only of the new marketing VDOM.

Next, we need to create a link between the two VDOM's," **marketing**" and "**root**", so they can connect and the traffic can move from the marketing LAN interface to the root VDOM and from there to the internet.

Again, let's move to global VDOM ----- network interfaces.

And here we will create what is known as a VDOM link, which is a link between VDOM's

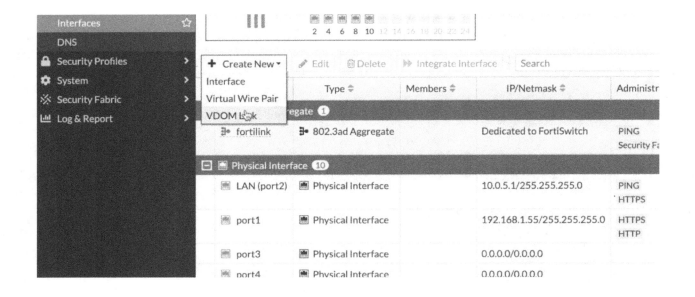

We will name our link "inter link" . And it will come from the root VDOM towards the marketing and vice versa.

We need to create a point to point links. So let's create two IP addresses in NAT mode 192 168.5.1/30. We will enable HTTPS and SSH, and the second link will be 192 168.5.2/30. So we can have a point-to-point connection.

Now we have a VDOM Link connection between the two VDOM's

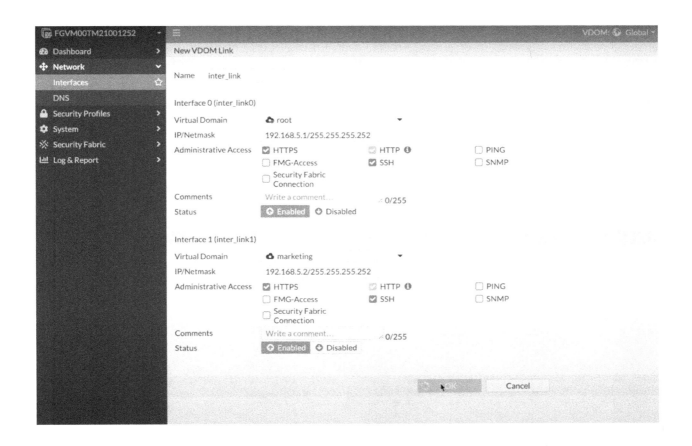

As you can see, those two links are labeled the first one is link zero and the second one is link one

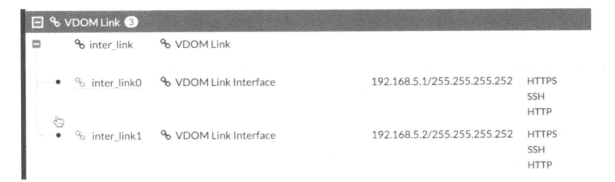

We need to enable the static route, so traffic can move from one route to the second.

Let's start with the first static route on our marketing VDOM

Move to network ---- static route and configure

We will create a default route that will actually forward any traffic towards our root gateway which is at 192 168.5.1. And the interface is InterLink1.

New Static Route

Destination ❶	[Subnet] Internet Service
	0.0.0.0/0.0.0.0
Gateway Address	192.168.5.1
Interface	⌗ inter_link1 ▼
Administrative Distance ❶	10 ⇕
Comments	Write a comment... ⟋ 0/255
Status	[⬆ Enabled] ⬇ Disabled

➕ Advanced Options

We have a static route in our marketing video. let's move to our route VDOM And create another static route.

This time it will not be a default route. we will create a route that is actually destined to our port 2 which is the LAN interface (10.0.5.0 subnet) on our marketing division.

The gateway address is 192 168.5.2. That is the other side of our inter VLAN link and, and the interface is inter Link 0.

New Static Route

Destination ℹ	**Subnet** Internet Service
	10.0.5.0/24
Gateway Address	192.168.5.2
Interface	⌘ inter_link0 ▾
Administrative Distance ℹ	10
Comments	Write a comment... 0/255
Status	⬆ **Enabled** ⬇ Disabled

➕ Advanced Options

Now we have a static route towards our LAN Interface on our marketing VDOM. And in our marketing VDOM, we have another static route that actually leads to 192 168 5.1. That is the other side of our Virtual link.

The last thing is the firewall policy

Move to Policy and objects---firewall policy

Name Your Policy **"full access"**

The incoming interface is our LAN interface. That's our marketing division, The outgoing interface is our interlink 1, source can be all, the destination can be all service can be all, since they're connected, we do not need NAT and you can apply any security profile.

New Policy

Name 🛈	full access
Incoming Interface	▦ LAN (port2) ▾
Outgoing Interface	⚭ inter_link1 ▾
Source	▤ all ✕
	✚
Destination	▤ all ✕
	✚
Schedule	🕓 always ▾
Service	▣ ALL ✕
	✚
Action	✔ ACCEPT ⊘ DENY

Inspection Mode [Flow-based] Proxy-based

Firewall / Network Options

NAT ⬤◯

Protocol Options [PROT] default ▾ ✎

Security Profiles

Now, move to the root VDOM, let's create the firewall policy on the other side. Name it **"full access"**, the incoming interface is our interlink 0, and the outgoing interface is our port one, port one is our WAN interface that's the upstream link that is connected to our ISP router.

The source will be all, destination all, service all, and here we will use the NAT since we are going to the internet and we need to NAT our Traffic.

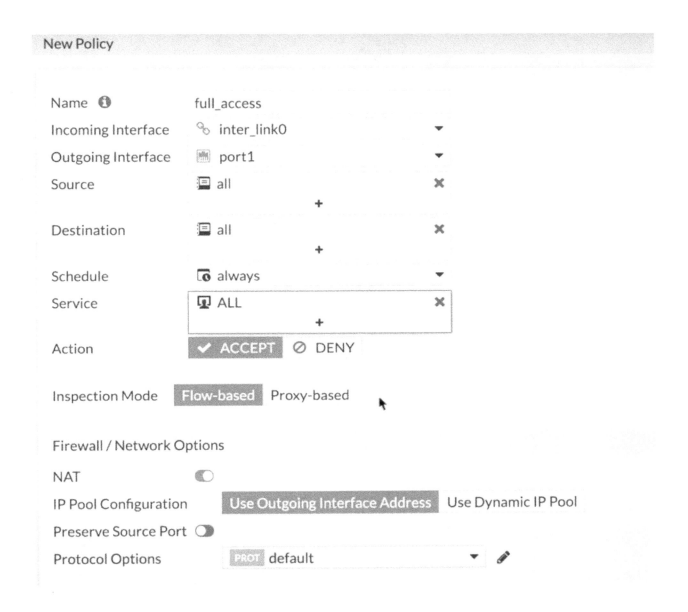

let's move back to our marketing VDOM and it seems that we are all set.

You can check That everything works well, using the execute ping command . one thing to note, whenever you wish to execute commands on the CLI, write down first

Config vdom

Edit <your vdom name>

Final **Words**

You have just Finished "Fortigate Admin Crash Course " Part 1

I hope that you enjoyed the journey. My aim was to give you a head start on the task of administering one of the best next-generation firewalls in the market.

But this was just the beginning. Your Fortigate firewall has so many areas that we have not touched upon as Vdom's, Proxies, security profiles, inspection modes, clustering, and much more

"Fortigate Security crash course" is in the work and soon be published

Sincerely yours

Ofer Shmueli

www.ingramcontent.com/pod-product-compliance
Lightning Source LLC
LaVergne TN
LVHW081757050326
832903LV00027B/1978